NINJA CREAMI HIGH-PROTEIN MAX POWER COOKBOOK

2000 Days of Delicious, Protein-Packed Frozen Treats with Unique Flavors to Fuel Your Healthy Lifestyle | Full Color Edition

Kelly R. Bonilla

Manufactured in the United States of America
Interior and Cover Designer: Danielle Rees
Art Producer: Brooke White
Editor: Aaliyah Lyons
Production Editor: Sienna Adams
Production Manager: Sarah Johnson
Photography: Michael Smith

TABLE OF CONTENTS

TABLE OF CONTENTS

INTRODUCTION

Growing up, I always loved ice cream, but as a busy mom of two active teenagers, I started looking at treats differently. My kids are always rushing between soccer practice, dance classes, and school activities, and I wanted to give them something delicious that actually fuels their bodies.

It all started one summer when my son Jake came home from football training complaining about bland protein shakes. "Mom," he said, "there's got to be a better way to get protein!" That's when the lightbulb went off. What if we could transform boring protein supplements into something we'd actually get excited about?

Enter the Ninja CREAMi. This little machine became our family's nutrition game-changer. We started experimenting—Greek yogurt, protein powder, fresh fruits, and just a touch of natural sweetener. Suddenly, dessert wasn't just a treat; it was a powerful post-workout recovery meal. My daughter Emma, a competitive dancer, was especially thrilled. She could now enjoy a creamy, delicious dessert that actually supported her muscle recovery.

This cookbook is our family's journey of turning "healthy" from a chore into a celebration.

DEDICATION

Our kitchen was always filled with laughter, despite our failures during our recipe adventures. Burnt edges, lumpy mixtures, and ice cream that looked more like soup became our shared memories. Jake would dramatically announce each "epic fail" while Emma rolled her eyes and giggled. My husband would just shake his head, grabbing a spoon and declaring, "It all tastes the same!" Those messy moments taught us something valuable—perfection isn't the goal. Connection is. Every splattered counter and failed recipe brought us closer, turning our kitchen into a playground of creativity and unconditional love.

CHAPTER 1: UNLOCKING THE POWER OF THE NINJA CREAMI

WHY HIGH-PROTEIN MATTERS

Protein is one of the most essential macronutrients, playing a crucial role in nearly every function of the body. Whether you're an athlete looking to build muscle, someone aiming to maintain a healthy weight, or simply focused on overall well-being, a high-protein diet offers numerous benefits. with the Ninja CREAMi, you can create delicious, protein-packed treats that make it easier to meet your daily protein goals while enjoying creamy, satisfying flavors.

The Benefits of a High-Protein Diet

Λ high-protein diet offers several advantages, particularly when incorporated into desserts and frozen treats. One of the biggest benefits is satiety and appetite control. Protein helps keep you full longer, reducing cravings and making it easier to manage your overall food intake. This makes high-protein ice cream a fantastic option for those looking to maintain a healthy weight while enjoying a sweet, satisfying treat.

Another major advantage of protein-rich diets is their role in metabolism and muscle maintenance. Protein has a higher thermic effect than fats or carbohydrates, meaning your body burns more calories digesting and processing it. Additionally, consuming enough protein helps prevent muscle loss, which is especially important when dieting or as you age.

Unlike traditional ice cream, which is often packed with sugar and lacks nutritional value, high-protein ice cream can be a healthier alternative. By using Greek yogurt, cottage cheese, protein powders, and milk alternatives, you can create creamy, delicious frozen desserts that fuel your body while satisfying your sweet tooth.

How Protein Supports Muscle Growth and Recovery

Protein is essential for muscle recovery and growth, making it a great addition to post-workout meals. After exercise, your muscles need amino acids to repair and rebuild stronger. A high-protein ice cream made with whey or casein protein can be a perfect way to refuel while indulging in something delicious.

Whey protein is a fast-digesting protein that quickly delivers amino acids to your muscles, making it ideal for post-workout recovery. On the other hand, casein protein digests more slowly, providing a steady release of nutrients that can help keep your muscles nourished for longer periods—making it a great option for a nighttime treat.

For those who prefer plant-based protein sources, pea protein, soy protein, or almond-based protein powders are excellent alternatives. When blended with ingredients like frozen bananas, unsweetened almond milk, or coconut yogurt, these proteins can create rich and creamy frozen treats that support muscle repair while catering to dairy-free lifestyles.

Finding the Right Protein Sources for Your Ninja CREAMi Creations

When making high-protein frozen desserts, it's important to choose ingredients that not only boost protein content but also enhance texture and flavor. Here are some of the best protein sources for your Ninja CREAMi creations:

- **Protein Powders:** Whey, casein, and plant-based options like pea or soy protein mix well into frozen treats, providing an easy way to increase protein without altering taste significantly.

- **Greek Yogurt:** A naturally high-protein dairy option that adds creaminess and tangy flavor while keeping desserts smooth.

- **Cottage Cheese:** Blends into an ultra-smooth consistency when frozen and churned, offering a protein-rich base with a naturally creamy texture.

- **Fairlife Milk or Ultra-Filtered Milk:** These dairy options have higher protein content than regular milk, making them great for boosting the nutritional value of your frozen treats.

GETTING TO KNOW YOUR NINJA CREAMI

The Ninja CREAMi is a revolutionary kitchen appliance that allows you to create creamy, delicious frozen treats at home with ease. Whether you're making high-protein ice cream, sorbets, or frozen smoothies, understanding the key features, selecting the best ingredients, and mastering pro tips will ensure you get the most out of this powerful machine. Here's a breakdown of everything you need to know to make the most of your Ninja CREAMi.

Key Features and Functions for Maximum Performance

The Ninja CREAMi is designed to make frozen desserts smoother and creamier than traditional methods. One of its standout features is the creami-fying process, where frozen ingredients are processed using a fine blade that transforms them into a soft-serve-like consistency. It's perfect for creating everything from decadent high-protein ice creams to refreshing sorbets.

Multiple settings are built into the Ninja CREAMi for different types of frozen treats. For example, the "Ice Cream" setting is designed for thick, rich results, while the "Sorbet" setting helps achieve a lighter, fluffier texture perfect for fruit-based frozen treats. There's also a "Milkshake" setting, which whips up smooth, milkshake-like textures. Using the right setting for the type of treat you want ensures that you achieve optimal results with every use.

The wide, easy-to-fill pint containers and the storage lids are practical additions, letting you make and store your creations all in one container. The Ninja CREAMi also features easy-to-clean components, with dishwasher-safe parts that make cleanup a breeze after you enjoy your homemade frozen delights.

Choosing the Best Ingredients for Perfect Textures

For the perfect frozen treat, ingredient selection is key. The Ninja CREAMi excels when using a variety of ingredients, but the texture and consistency depend heavily on the type of base you choose.

High-protein bases like Greek yogurt, cottage cheese, or protein powders are excellent options for making indulgent yet nutritious ice cream. Greek yogurt, in particular, creates a thick, creamy consistency while adding a tangy flavor that pairs well with sweeteners like honey or stevia. If you want an even richer texture, heavy cream or coconut cream can also be used to add extra smoothness and flavor.

When using fruit-based ingredients, like in sorbets or smoothies, it's important to use frozen fruit. Freezing the fruit ensures it blends seamlessly and results in the perfect frozen texture. For an ultra-smooth finish, consider blending fruits with a creamy base, such as yogurt or silken tofu, to enhance the consistency.

For plant-based options, unsweetened almond milk, cashew milk, or oat milk are great choices. These milks work well to create a creamy base while being dairy-free. Adding a thickening agent like guar gum or xanthan gum can also help improve the texture and ensure your ice cream doesn't turn icy once it's frozen.

Sweeteners can play a large role in the texture as

well. For a low-sugar option, try using erythritol, monk fruit, or stevia. These alternatives add sweetness without spiking your blood sugar. Just keep in mind that too much of certain sweeteners (especially erythritol) can affect the texture, so use them sparingly.

Pro Tips for Consistently Creamy Results

Achieving creamy, smooth, and consistent results with your Ninja CREAMi is easy once you understand the key techniques.

Pre-freezing is essential: Before using the Ninja CREAMi, make sure your base is properly frozen. The CREAMi works best when your mixture is fully frozen in the pint container for at least 24 hours. This ensures the ingredients freeze evenly, giving you that perfectly creamy texture when processed.

Don't overload the pint container: While it might be tempting to pack in a large batch, overfilling the pint can affect the texture and the machine's ability to process the mixture effectively. Follow the recommended fill lines to ensure smooth, creamy results.

Re-spin if necessary: If you find that your frozen treat isn't as creamy as you'd like, don't be afraid to re-spin it. The Ninja CREAMi has a built-in re-spin function, allowing you to process your mixture a second time for a smoother, creamier texture. This is especially useful when using high-protein ingredients or frozen fruits, which may need an extra spin to reach the desired consistency.

Experiment with mix-ins: The Ninja CREAMi also lets you mix in extra ingredients like chocolate chips, nuts, or fruit after the initial process. Simply add them into the mixture after the first spin, then use the "Mix-In" setting for a few seconds to incorporate them evenly.

MASTERING HIGH-PROTEIN CREAMI CREATIONS

Creating the perfect high-protein frozen treats with the Ninja CREAMi is all about finding the right balance between flavor, texture, and nutrition. with the ability to easily blend healthy ingredients into creamy desserts, this appliance is a game-changer for anyone looking to enjoy protein-packed ice creams, smoothies, or sorbets without sacrificing taste. Here's how to perfect your high-protein CREAMi creations for the best results every time.

Creative Mix-Ins and Toppings for Extra Boosts

Once you've perfected your high-protein base, the fun begins with creative mix-ins and toppings. The Ninja CREAMi allows you to add these ingredients after the first spin, giving you total control over the final texture. These additions not only boost the nutritional content but can also elevate the flavor and texture of your frozen treat.

Nuts and seeds are excellent mix-ins that add crunch and a healthy dose of fat, protein, and fiber. Try adding almonds, walnuts, chia seeds, or flaxseeds for a nutritious and satisfying boost. Nuts and seeds pair well with nearly any flavor, from chocolate and vanilla to fruit-based ice creams. Just remember to chop them into smaller pieces to avoid disrupting the smooth texture of your frozen treat.

If you're a fan of indulgence, chocolate chips, cacao nibs, or swirlable peanut butter can create a more decadent treat. Choose dark chocolate chips for a healthier option that packs antioxidants and pairs well with high-protein ice cream.

For added flavor, fruit is a great choice. Fresh or frozen berries, such as strawberries, raspberries, or blueberries, mix well into yogurt or protein ice cream. For a tropical twist, try adding diced mango or pineapple for a refreshing, vibrant flavor. These fruity mix-ins not only add natural sweetness but are packed with vitamins and fiber.

To top off your high-protein creations, consider a dollop of whipped cream, granola, or a drizzle of honey (if you prefer a little extra sweetness). A sprinkle of cinnamon, cocoa powder, or shredded coconut also adds texture and a burst of flavor to any frozen treat.

Avoiding Common Pitfalls for the Best Results Every Time

While making high-protein frozen desserts with the Ninja CREAMi is a lot of fun, there are a few common mistakes to watch out for that can affect the final results.

One of the most common pitfalls is under-freezing your base. For the best results, make sure your mixture is fully frozen before processing. If you skip the freezing step or don't allow enough time, the texture can end up too soft or watery. Ensure the base is frozen for at least 24 hours before spinning it in the Ninja CREAMi for optimal texture.

Another mistake to avoid is overloading the pint container. The Ninja CREAMi works best when the container is filled to the recommended line. Too much or too little mixture can affect the spinning process, resulting in uneven textures. Stick to the recommended amount for consistent, smooth results every time.

When adding mix-ins, avoid adding too many hard or chunky ingredients that could make the texture uneven or disrupt the creaminess. For example, adding large pieces of frozen fruit or oversized chocolate chunks might prevent the machine from properly processing the mixture. It's best to chop mix-ins into smaller pieces and add them in moderation.

Lastly, don't skip the re-spin function. Sometimes, after the first spin, your high-protein frozen treat may need a little more processing to reach the perfect consistency. If the texture is too dense or icy, simply use the re-spin feature to achieve a smoother, creamier result.

Q&A for Ninja CREAMi Beginners

Q: Can I use non-dairy milk in the Ninja CREAMi for high-protein recipes?

A: Yes, you can absolutely use non-dairy milk in your Ninja CREAMi. Options like almond milk, cashew milk, and oat milk work great, especially for dairy-free or vegan high-protein treats. To achieve a creamy texture, choose unsweetened versions and consider adding a little bit of coconut cream or avocado for added richness. These non-dairy milks blend well with protein powder and help create a smooth, creamy base without sacrificing flavor.

Q: How do I get rid of ice crystals in my frozen treats?

A: Ice crystals can form if the mixture isn't frozen properly. To avoid this, make sure your base is completely frozen for at least 24 hours before processing in the Ninja CREAMi. Additionally, if you're using high-protein ingredients like Greek yogurt or cottage cheese, make sure they're well-blended before freezing. Adding a small amount of thickening agents (like xanthan gum) can also help achieve a smoother, creamier consistency and prevent ice crystals from forming.

Q: What's the best way to make a protein-packed smoothie bowl in the Ninja CREAMi?

A: Making a high-protein smoothie bowl is easy! Start with a thick base like Greek yogurt or silken tofu. Add your favorite protein powder, then freeze the mixture in the Ninja CREAMi pint for 24 hours. Once frozen, use the "Smoothie Bowl" setting to achieve a thicker texture perfect for topping with fruit, nuts, or granola. For an extra protein boost, add some chia seeds or hemp hearts as toppings.

Q: Can I make dairy-free high-protein ice cream in the Ninja CREAMi?

A: Definitely! To make dairy-free high-protein ice cream, choose plant-based protein powder (like pea protein or hemp protein), and use a non-dairy milk like coconut milk or almond milk. For richness, you can add coconut cream or avocado to help with creaminess. Don't forget to freeze the mixture properly before processing, and use the "Ice Cream" setting for the best texture.

CHAPTER 2: ICE CREAM RECIPES

MANGO ICE CREAM

Prep time: 10 minutes | Cook time: 10 minutes | Serves 4

- ¼ cup granulated sugar
- 1 tablespoon cream cheese, softened
- 1 cup whole milk
- ¾ cup heavy whipping cream
- 2 ripe mangoes, diced into small cubes

1. In a medium bowl, mix the sugar and softened cream cheese until well combined.
2. Add the milk and heavy whipping cream. Whisk until completely blended.
3. Transfer the mixture into a clean Ninja CREAMi Pint container.
4. Add the mango cubes and gently stir to distribute evenly.
5. Secure the container with the storage lid and freeze for 24 hours or until completely solid.
6. After 24 hours, remove the lid. Place the pint in the outer bowl of the Ninja CREAMi.
7. Insert the Creamerizer Paddle and lock the outer bowl lid in place. Insert the bowl into the Ninja CREAMi base.
8. Select the ICE CREAM button and press start.
9. When the program is complete, twist the outer bowl to unlock it from the machine and remove.
10. Scoop and serve immediately or store with the storage lid for later enjoyment.

Per Serving

Calories: 265 | Fat: 11g | Carbs: 41g | Fiber: 2.7g | Protein: 4g

PEANUT BUTTER AND GRAPE JELLY ICE CREAM

Prep time: 25 minutes | Cook time: 15 minutes | Serves 4

- 4 large egg yolks
- ⅓ cup heavy cream
- ¼ cup smooth peanut butter
- ¼ cup honey roasted peanuts, chopped
- 3 tablespoons granulated sugar
- 1 cup whole milk
- 3 tablespoons grape jelly

1. In a small saucepan over low heat, whisk together the egg yolks and sugar until well combined.
2. Add the heavy cream, milk, peanut butter, and grape jelly. Whisk until smooth.
3. Cook over medium-low heat, stirring constantly, until the mixture reaches 175°F on a candy thermometer.
4. Remove from heat and allow to cool completely to room temperature.
5. Pour the cooled mixture into a clean Ninja CREAMi pint container.
6. Secure the storage lid and freeze for 24 hours or until completely solid.
7. After 24 hours, remove the lid and place the pint in the Ninja CREAMi outer bowl. Insert the Creamerizer Paddle.
8. Secure the outer bowl lid, place the assembly on the Ninja CREAMi base, and lock it in place. Press the POWER button to turn on the unit, then select the ICE CREAM function.
9. When processing is complete, use a spoon to create a wide hole in the center of the ice cream that reaches the bottom of the pint.
10. Fill the hole with chopped honey roasted peanuts and select the MIX-IN function.
11. Once the MIX-IN cycle is complete, scoop the ice cream into serving bowls and enjoy.

Per Serving

Calories: 340 | Fat: 22g | Carbs: 26g | Fiber: 1g | Protein: 11g

CINAMON BUN ICE CREAM

Prep Time: 10 minutes | Cook time: 10 minutes | Serves 2

- 1 cup whole milk
- 1 teaspoon vanilla extract
- 1 teaspoon ground cinnamon
- 1 tablespoon cream cheese, softened
- 2½ tablespoons raw agave nectar
- ¾ cup heavy cream

1. In a microwave-safe bowl, heat cream cheese for 10 seconds to soften. Using a spatula, mix in the agave nectar, vanilla extract, and ground cinnamon until smooth and creamy (about 1 minute).
2. Gradually whisk in the heavy cream and milk until the mixture is fully combined and smooth.
3. Pour the mixture into a clean Ninja CREAMi pint container, leaving ½ inch of space at the top.
4. Secure the storage lid and place the container in the freezer for 24 hours.
5. After 24 hours, remove the pint from the freezer and take off the storage lid.
6. Place the pint in the Ninja CREAMi outer bowl, then insert the Creamerizer Paddle.
7. Secure the outer bowl lid and place the assembled bowl onto the motor base. Lock it in place by turning the handle to the right.
8. Select the LIGHT ICE CREAM function and press start.
9. When processing is complete, unlock the bowl from the base and remove. Serve immediately for best texture.

Per Serving

Calories: 473 | Fat: 39.5g | Carbs: 25.3g | Fiber: 0.7g | Protein: 7g

BURNT SUGAR ICE CREAM

Prep time: 15 minutes | Cook time: 15 minutes | Serves 4

- 1 cup unsweetened soy milk
- 3 prepared vegan egg replacer (equivalent to 3 eggs)
- ½ cup unsweetened plant-based creamer
- 1 pinch of kosher salt
- 1 tablespoon water
- ¼ cup packed dark brown sugar
- ¼ cup granulated sugar

1. In a medium bowl, whisk together the soy milk, brown sugar, plant-based creamer, salt, and prepared vegan egg replacer until well combined.
2. In a medium saucepan over medium heat, combine the granulated sugar and water.
3. Cook for about 5 minutes, stirring occasionally, until the mixture turns amber and caramelizes.
4. Carefully add the vegan egg mixture to the caramel, stirring gently. Remove from heat immediately.
5. Allow the mixture to cool slightly, then pour into a clean Ninja CREAMi pint container.
6. Secure the storage lid and freeze for 24 hours or until completely solid.
7. After 24 hours, remove the lid and place the pint in the Ninja CREAMi outer bowl.
8. Insert the Creamerizer Paddle and secure the outer bowl lid. Place the assembly onto the Ninja CREAMi base and lock in place.
9. Press the POWER button to turn on the unit, then select the ICE CREAM function.
10. When processing is complete, remove the ice cream from the pint and serve chilled.

Per Serving

Calories: 192 | Fat: 6g | Carbs: 27g | Fiber: 0.4g | Protein: 8.2g

VANILLA CORN ICE CREAM

Prep time: 10 minutes | Cook time: 5 minutes | Serves 1

- 1 cup cold milk
- ¼ tablespoon cornstarch
- ¼ cup heavy cream
- ¼ cup granulated sugar
- ½ teaspoon vanilla extract

1. In a small bowl, whisk together the cornstarch and 2 tablespoons of the cold milk to make a smooth slurry. (Using cold milk prevents lumps from forming.)
2. In a medium saucepan, combine the remaining milk, heavy cream, and sugar. Warm over medium-low heat, stirring until sugar dissolves.
3. Gradually whisk the cornstarch slurry into the warm milk mixture. Cook for 2-3 minutes, stirring constantly, until slightly thickened.
4. Remove from heat and stir in the vanilla extract. Let cool completely.
5. Pour the cooled mixture into a clean Ninja CREAMi Pint container, leaving ½ inch of space at the top.
6. Secure the storage lid and freeze for 24 hours or until completely solid.
7. After 24 hours, remove the Pint from the freezer and take off the lid.
8. Place the Ninja CREAMi Pint into the outer bowl, then insert the outer bowl into the Ninja CREAMi machine. Turn until the outer bowl locks into place.
9. Select the ICE CREAM button and press start. During processing, the mixture will transform into smooth, creamy ice cream.
10. Once the ICE CREAM function has completed, twist the outer bowl to release it from the Ninja CREAMi machine. Serve immediately for best texture.

Per Serving

Calories: 96 | Protein: 6g | Carbs: 18g | Fiber: 0.5g | Fat: 0.1g

CARAMEL ICE CREAM

Prep time: 15 minutes | Cook time: 10 minutes | Makes 2 pints

- 14 oz. canned dulce de leche
- 1¼ cups heavy cream
- 1 tablespoon bourbon (optional)

1. In the bowl of an electric mixer fitted with the whisk attachment, combine all ingredients.
2. Mix on medium speed until the mixture is thick and well combined, about 2-3 minutes.
3. Divide the mixture evenly between two Ninja CREAMi pint containers.
4. Secure the storage lids and freeze for at least 8 hours or until completely solid.
5. When ready to process, remove one container from the freezer and take off the lid.
6. Place the pint in the outer bowl and insert into the Ninja CREAMi machine.
7. Select the ICE CREAM function and press start.
8. Once processing is complete, remove the ice cream and repeat with the second container if desired.
9. For a softer consistency, use the RE-SPIN function if needed.

Per Serving

Calories: 1195 | Fat: 72.5g | Carbs: 114g | Fiber: 0g | Protein: 14g

PEANUT BUTTER ICE CREAM

Prep time: 10 minutes | Cook time: 15 minutes | Serves 4

- 1¾ cups skim milk
- 3 tablespoons smooth peanut butter
- ¼ cup stevia-cane sugar blend
- 1 teaspoon vanilla extract

1. In a medium bowl, combine all ingredients and whisk until smooth and well blended.
2. Let the mixture rest for about five minutes to allow flavors to incorporate.
3. Pour the mixture into a clean Ninja CREAMi pint container, leaving ½ inch of space at the top.
4. Secure the storage lid and freeze for 24 hours or until completely solid.
5. After 24 hours, remove the storage lid and place the pint in the Ninja CREAMi outer bowl.
6. Insert the Creamerizer Paddle into the outer bowl lid.
7. Secure the lid on the outer bowl by rotating it clockwise until it locks.
8. Place the assembly on the Ninja CREAMi base and lock it in place.
9. Press the POWER button to turn on the unit, then select the ICE CREAM function.
10. When processing is complete, twist the outer bowl to release it from the machine.
11. Scoop the ice cream into serving bowls and enjoy immediately for best texture.

Per Serving

Calories: 143 | Fat: 6.1g | Carbs: 19.7g | Fiber: 0.7g | Protein: 6.5g

SWEET LEMON ICE CREAM

Prep Time: 10 minutes | Cook time: 20 minutes | Serves 5

- 1 cup heavy whipping cream
- ½ cup half and half
- ½ cup granulated sugar
- 1 tablespoon lemon zest, freshly grated
- 2 egg yolks
- ¼ cup fresh lemon juice

1. In a medium saucepan over low heat, whisk together the heavy cream, half and half, sugar, and lemon zest until the sugar is completely dissolved (about 5 minutes).
2. In a separate bowl, whisk the egg yolks until smooth.
3. Gradually add a few tablespoons of the warm cream mixture to the egg yolks, whisking constantly. This tempers the eggs to prevent them from scrambling.
4. Slowly pour the egg mixture back into the saucepan with the remaining cream mixture, whisking constantly.
5. Cook over medium-low heat, stirring continuously for 5-10 minutes until the mixture thickens slightly and coats the back of a spoon.
6. Remove from heat and stir in the fresh lemon juice.
7. Allow the mixture to cool completely, then pour into a clean Ninja CREAMi pint container.
8. Secure the storage lid and freeze for 24 hours or until completely solid.
9. After 24 hours, remove the lid and place the pint in the Ninja CREAMi outer bowl.
10. Insert the Creamerizer Paddle, secure the outer bowl lid, and place the assembly on the Ninja CREAMi base. Lock it in place.
11. Press the POWER button, then select the ICE CREAM function.
12. When processing is complete, twist the outer bowl to release it from the machine and serve immediately.

Per Serving

Calories: 431 | Fat:6g | Carbs:32g | Protein:8g | Fiber: 0g

STRAWBERRY ICE CREAM

Prep time: 5 minutes | Cook time: 10 minutes | Makes 1 pint

- 1 tablespoon cream cheese, softened
- ¼ cup granulated sugar
- 1 teaspoon vanilla bean paste (or vanilla extract)
- ¾ cup heavy whipping cream
- 1 cup whole milk
- 6 fresh strawberries, sliced

1. In a medium bowl, combine the softened cream cheese and sugar. Whisk until smooth.
2. Add the vanilla bean paste, heavy whipping cream, and milk. Stir until completely combined.
3. Gently fold in the sliced strawberries.
4. Pour the mixture into a clean Ninja CREAMi pint container, leaving ½ inch of space at the top.
5. Secure the storage lid and freeze for 24 hours or until completely solid.
6. After 24 hours, remove the lid and place the pint in the Ninja CREAMi outer bowl.
7. Insert the Creamerizer Paddle, secure the outer bowl lid, and place the assembly on the Ninja CREAMi base.
8. Press the POWER button to turn on the unit, then select the ICE CREAM function.
9. When processing is complete, twist the outer bowl to release it from the machine. For extra smoothness, you can use the RE-SPIN function if needed.
10. Serve immediately or store with the storage lid for later enjoyment.

Per Serving

Calories: 1045 | Fat: 79.2g | Carbs: 74.3g | Fiber: 1.5g | Protein: 14.5g

TARO ICE CREAM

Prep time: 15 minutes | Cook time: 30 minutes | Serves 5

- 1 cup sweetened condensed milk
- ½ pound taro root, peeled
- 1 cup heavy cream, chilled

1. Cut the peeled taro root into 1-inch cubes. Place in a medium saucepan and cover with water.
2. Bring to a boil and cook for approximately 30 minutes or until the taro is fork-tender. Drain thoroughly.
3. In a food processor, puree the cooked taro until smooth.
4. In a medium bowl, combine the taro puree, heavy cream, and sweetened condensed milk. Mix until well blended.
5. Pour the mixture into a clean Ninja CREAMi pint container, leaving ½ inch of space at the top.
6. Secure the storage lid and freeze for 24 hours or until completely solid.
7. After 24 hours, remove the lid and place the pint in the Ninja CREAMi outer bowl. Insert the Creamerizer Paddle.
8. Secure the outer bowl lid, place the assembly on the Ninja CREAMi base, and lock it in place. Press the POWER button, then select the ICE CREAM function.
9. When processing is complete, scoop the ice cream into serving bowls and enjoy.

Per Serving

Calories: 330 | Fat: 14.3g | Carbs: 46g | Fiber: 1.9g | Protein: 6g

FROZEN HOT CHOCOLATE ICE CREAM

Prep time: 20 minutes | Cook time: 20 minutes | Makes 1 pint

- 1 cup chocolate milk
- ¼ cup half and half
- ¼ cup almond milk creamer
- 1 oz. hot cocoa mix (about 2 tablespoons)

1. In a medium microwave-safe bowl, combine the chocolate milk, half and half, and almond milk creamer.
2. Whisk until well blended.
3. Microwave the mixture for 2 minutes or until warm.
4. Add the hot cocoa mix and whisk until completely dissolved and smooth.
5. Allow the mixture to cool for 10 minutes, then pour into a clean Ninja CREAMi pint container.
6. Stir once more, then secure the storage lid.
7. Freeze for 24 hours or until completely solid.
8. After 24 hours, remove the lid and place the pint in the Ninja CREAMi outer bowl.
9. Insert the Creamerizer Paddle, secure the outer bowl lid, and place the assembly on the Ninja CREAMi base.
10. Press the POWER button, then select the ICE CREAM function.
11. When processing is complete, twist the outer bowl to release it from the machine. For extra smoothness, you can use the RE-SPIN function if needed.
12. Serve immediately topped with whipped cream and chocolate shavings if desired.

Per Serving

Calories: 355 | Protein: 10.84 | Fat: 8.32 | Carbs: 63.65 | Fiber: 1g

BLUEBERRY ICE CREAM

Prep time: 10 minutes | Cook time: 10 minutes | Serves 6

- 1 cup whole milk
- 6 mini pie crusts, crumbled (or graham cracker crust equivalent)
- ¾ cup heavy cream
- 1 large egg, beaten
- ¾ cup frozen blueberries, thawed and divided
- 1/3 cup granulated sugar

1. In a blender, combine half of the thawed blueberries with the milk, heavy cream, egg, sugar, and crumbled pie crusts. Blend until smooth.
2. Pour the mixture into a clean Ninja CREAMi pint container, leaving ½ inch of space at the top.
3. Secure the storage lid and freeze for 24 hours or until completely solid.
4. After 24 hours, remove the lid and place the pint in the Ninja CREAMi outer bowl. Insert the Creamerizer Paddle.
5. Secure the outer bowl lid, place the assembly on the Ninja CREAMi base, and lock it in place. Press the POWER button, then select the ICE CREAM function.
6. When processing is complete, use a spoon to create a wide hole in the center of the ice cream that reaches the bottom of the pint.
7. Add the remaining thawed blueberries to the hole and select the MIX-IN function.
8. Once the MIX-IN cycle is complete, scoop the ice cream into serving bowls and enjoy!

Per Serving

Calories: 1095 | Fat: 70g | Carbs: 103.3g | Fiber: 3.4g | Protein: 14.3g

BROWNIE CHOCOLATE CHIP ICE CREAM

Prep time: 15 minutes | Cook time: 15 minutes | Serves 2

- 2 large eggs
- 2 cups heavy cream
- ¼ cup smooth peanut butter
- ¾ cup granulated sugar
- 1 cup whole milk
- 1 cup mini chocolate chips
- ¼ cup chocolate chunks
- ¼ cup brownie pieces (store-bought or homemade)

1. In a blender, combine the eggs, sugar, heavy cream, milk, and peanut butter. Blend until smooth and well incorporated.
2. Stir in the mini chocolate chips by hand.
3. Refrigerate the mixture for at least one hour to allow flavors to meld.
4. Pour the chilled mixture into a clean Ninja CREAMi pint container, leaving ½ inch of space at the top.
5. Secure the storage lid and freeze for 24 hours or until completely solid.
6. After 24 hours, remove the lid and place the pint in the Ninja CREAMi outer bowl. Insert the Creamerizer Paddle.
7. Secure the outer bowl lid, place the assembly on the Ninja CREAMi base, and lock it in place. Press the POWER button, then select the ICE CREAM function.
8. When processing is complete, use a spoon to create a wide hole in the center of the ice cream that reaches the bottom of the pint.
9. Fill the hole with chocolate chunks and brownie pieces, then select the MIX-IN function.
10. Once the MIX-IN cycle is complete, scoop the ice cream into serving bowls and enjoy!

Per Serving

Calories: 1071 | Fat: 71.2g | Carbs: 97.5g | Fiber: 1.9g | Protein: 20.5g

PUMPKIN CHEESECAKE ICE CREAM

Prep time: 10 minutes | Cook time: 5 minutes | Makes 1 pint

- 8 oz. cream cheese, softened
- 1 cup heavy cream
- ¼ cup pumpkin puree (not pumpkin pie filling)
- ½ cup packed brown sugar
- 1 teaspoon vanilla extract
- ½ teaspoon pumpkin pie spice

1. Place the cream cheese in a microwave-safe bowl and microwave for 30 seconds to soften it completely.
2. Add the heavy cream, pumpkin puree, brown sugar, vanilla extract, and pumpkin pie spice to the bowl with the softened cream cheese.
3. Whisk until smooth and fully combined. For a smoother mixture, you can use a hand mixer on medium speed.
4. Pour the mixture into a clean Ninja CREAMi pint container, leaving ½ inch of space at the top.
5. Secure the storage lid and freeze for 24 hours or until completely solid.
6. After 24 hours, remove the lid and place the pint in the Ninja CREAMi outer bowl.
7. Insert the Creamerizer Paddle, secure the outer bowl lid, and place the assembly onto the Ninja CREAMi base. Lock it in place.
8. Press the POWER button, then select the ICE CREAM function.
9. When processing is complete, twist the outer bowl to release it from the machine. For extra smoothness, you can use the RE-SPIN function if needed.
10. Serve immediately topped with crushed graham crackers or gingersnaps if desired.

Per Serving

Calories: 1686 | Protein: 27.55 | Fat: 123.85 | Carbs: 124.68 | Fiber: 0.5g

COOKIES AND CREAM CUSTARD ICE CREAM

Prep time: 15 minutes | **Cook time:** 10 minutes | **Serves** 4

- 10 chocolate sandwich cookies (like Oreos), roughly chopped
- 1 cup heavy cream
- ½ cup granulated sugar
- ½ cup whole milk
- 1 teaspoon vanilla extract
- 3 egg yolks
- ⅛ teaspoon salt

1. In a medium saucepan, combine ¼ cup of sugar with ½ cup milk and salt. Heat over medium heat until it just begins to simmer, then remove from heat.
2. In a separate bowl, whisk together the egg yolks with the remaining ¼ cup sugar and milk until well blended.
3. Gradually add a small amount of the hot milk mixture to the egg mixture, whisking constantly to temper the eggs.
4. Pour the tempered egg mixture back into the saucepan and cook over medium-low heat for about 5 minutes, stirring constantly, until the mixture thickens enough to coat the back of a spoon.
5. Remove from heat and allow to cool completely.
6. Once cooled, stir in the heavy cream, vanilla extract, and chopped cookies.
7. Pour the mixture into a clean Ninja CREAMi pint container, leaving ½ inch of space at the top.
8. Secure the storage lid and freeze for 24 hours or until completely solid.
9. After 24 hours, remove the lid and place the pint in the Ninja CREAMi outer bowl. Insert the Creamerizer Paddle.
10. Secure the outer bowl lid, place the assembly on the Ninja CREAMi base, and lock it in place. Press the POWER button, then select the ICE CREAM function.
11. When processing is complete, scoop the ice cream into serving bowls and enjoy!

Per Serving

Calories: 2109 | **Fat:** 105.5g | **Carbs:** 257.8g | **Fiber:** 2.5g | **Protein:** 43.6g

CHAPTER 3: GELATO RECIPES

BLACK CHERRY GELATO

Prep time: 40 minutes | Cook time: 15 minutes | Makes 1 pint

- 4 egg yolks
- 5 tablespoons granulated sugar
- 1 tablespoon corn syrup
- 1 cup heavy cream
- ⅓ cup whole milk
- 1 teaspoon almond extract
- 1 cup black cherries, pitted and sliced

1. Add the egg yolks, sugar, and corn syrup to a saucepan and whisk until well combined.
2. Stir in the heavy cream, almond extract, and milk.
3. Place the pan over medium heat.
4. Cook, stirring continuously, until the temperature reaches 165°F (use a candy thermometer).
5. Strain the mixture through a fine-mesh strainer into the Ninja CREAMi pint container.
6. Allow to cool completely, then cover with the storage lid.
7. Freeze for 24 hours or until completely solid.
8. Remove the lid and place the pint container in the outer bowl of the Ninja CREAMi.
9. Secure the Creamerizer Paddle and lid.
10. Select the GELATO function.
11. Once processing is complete, serve immediately.

Per Serving

Calories: **932** | Protein: **16.7** | Fat: **66.06** | Carbs: **71.54** | Fiber: **1g**

LITE APPLE PIE ICE CREAM

Prep Time: 10 minutes | Cook time: 12 minutes | Serves 2

- ½ teaspoon cinnamon
- 2 cups apples, peeled and chopped
- 1 teaspoon vanilla extract
- 3 tablespoons brown sugar
- ½ cup heavy cream
- ½ cup apple cider
- Nonstick cooking spray

1. Spray a medium saucepan with nonstick cooking spray and place over medium heat.
2. Add the chopped apples with 3 tablespoons of water. Cook for about 10 minutes, or until the apples are soft and the water has evaporated.
3. Add brown sugar, vanilla, and cinnamon to the saucepan. Cook for an additional 2-3 minutes, or until the apples are completely soft.
4. Transfer the cooked apple mixture to a large mixing bowl, then thoroughly combine with the heavy cream and apple cider.
5. Pour the mixture into a clean Ninja CREAMi pint container.
6. Place the pint container in an ice bath to cool completely.
7. Once cooled, cover the pint with the storage lid and freeze for 24 hours.
8. Remove the pint from the freezer and take off the lid.
9. Place the pint in the Ninja CREAMi outer bowl, secure the lid component to the outer bowl, and attach the Creamerizer Paddle to the lid.
10. Place the bowl assembly on the motor base and twist the handle to the right to raise and lock the platform in place.
11. Select the GELATO function.
12. Once processing is complete, scoop the ice cream out of the pint and serve immediately.

Per Serving

Calories: **144** | Fat:**6g** | Carbs:**15g** | Protein:**12g** | Fiber: **4g**

CHERRY GELATO

Prep time: 6 minutes | Cook time: 3 minutes | Serves 4

- 4 large egg yolks
- 1 tablespoon light corn syrup
- 5 tablespoons granulated sugar
- 1 cup heavy cream
- ⅓ cup whole milk
- 1 teaspoon almond extract
- 1 cup frozen black cherries, pitted and quartered

1. In a small saucepan, add the egg yolks, sugar, and corn syrup and whisk until well combined.
2. Add the heavy cream, milk, and almond extract and whisk until well combined.
3. Place the saucepan over medium heat and cook for about 2-3 minutes, stirring continuously.
4. Remove from the heat and strain the mixture through a fine-mesh strainer into an empty Ninja CREAMi pint container.
5. Place the container into an ice bath to cool completely.
6. After cooling, cover the container with the storage lid and freeze for 24 hours.
7. After 24 hours, remove the lid from container and place it into the outer bowl of the Ninja CREAMi.
8. Install the Creamerizer Paddle onto the lid of the outer bowl.
9. Secure the outer bowl onto the motor base and rotate the handle clockwise to lock it in place.
10. Press the POWER button to turn on the unit.
11. Press the GELATO button.
12. When the program is completed, use a spoon to create a 1½-inch wide hole in the center that reaches the bottom of the pint container.
13. Add the cherries into the hole and press the MIX-IN button.
14. When the program is completed, turn the outer bowl and release it from the machine.
15. Transfer the gelato into serving bowls and serve immediately.

Per Serving

Calories:271| Fat:12g | Carbs:2g | Protein:11g | Fiber: 4g

TROPICAL COCONUT RUM AND COKE GELATO

Prep time: 5 minutes | Cook time: 30 minutes | Serves 4-6

- ½ cup heavy cream
- 2 cups milk
- 3/4 cup sugar
- 1 teaspoon vanilla extract
- 3 tablespoons rum
- ¼ cup shaved coconut
- 3 cups coca cola (2, 12 ounce cans)

1. Pour the coke into a large skillet, and heat it on high heat until it comes to a boil. Allow the coke to cook for about another 15 or 20 minutes, until the coke reduces down to 1 cup of liquid. Let the liquid cool.
2. Place the milk and cream in a bowl, and mix them together until well combined. Use a whisk to mix in the sugar. Continue to whisk for about 4 minutes until the sugar dissolves. Then mix in the vanilla extract, coke reduction, coconut chips and rum.
3. Pour the ingredients into your Ninja CREAMi, and Press the GELATO button. Let it churn for 25 minutes.
4. Put the gelato in an airtight container and place in the freezer for up to 2 hours, until desired consistency is reached.

Per Serving

Calories: 335 | Fat: 11g | Carbs: 31g | Fiber: 1g | Protein: 7g

BLUEBERRY & GRAHAM CRACKER GELATO

Prep time: 10 minutes | Cook time: 3 minutes | Serves 4

- 4 large egg yolks
- 3 tablespoons granulated sugar
- 3 tablespoons wild blueberry preserves
- 1 teaspoon vanilla extract
- 1 cup whole milk
- ⅓ cup heavy cream
- ¼ cup cream cheese, softened
- 3-6 drops purple food coloring
- 2 large graham crackers, broken into 1-inch pieces

1. In a small saucepan, whisk together the egg yolks, sugar, blueberry preserves, and vanilla extract until well combined.
2. Add the milk, heavy cream, cream cheese, and food coloring, and whisk until well combined.
3. Place the saucepan over medium heat and cook for about 2-3 minutes, stirring continuously, until the mixture slightly thickens.
4. Remove from the heat and strain the mixture through a fine-mesh strainer into an empty Ninja CREAMi pint.
5. Place the pint in an ice bath to cool completely.
6. After cooling, cover the pint with the storage lid and freeze for 24 hours.
7. After 24 hours, remove the lid from the frozen pint and place it into the Ninja CREAMi outer bowl.
8. Install the Creamerizer Paddle onto the outer bowl lid.
9. Rotate the lid clockwise to lock it onto the outer bowl.
10. Press the Power button to turn on the unit.
11. Press the GELATO button.
12. When the program is complete, use a spoon to create a 1 ½-inch wide hole in the center of the gelato, reaching the bottom of the pint.
13. Add the graham cracker pieces into the hole and press the MIX-IN button.
14. When the program is complete, remove the outer bowl from the machine.
15. Transfer the gelato into serving bowls and serve immediately.

Per Serving

Calories: 230 | Fat: 15g | Carbs: 24g | Fiber: 1g | Protein: 5g

PUMPKIN PIE SQUASH GELATO

Prep Time: 10 minutes | Cook time: 5 minutes | Serves 2

- ½ cup cooked butternut squash
- ¼ cup granulated sugar
- Pinch of salt
- ¼ teaspoon allspice
- 1 ¾ cups milk
- ½ teaspoon cinnamon

1. In a small saucepan, mix all ingredients and heat over medium heat for 5 minutes, or until the sugar dissolves.
2. Pour the mixture into an empty Ninja CREAMi pint.

Secure the storage lid and freeze for 24 hours.

3. Remove the frozen pint from the freezer. Place the pint in the Ninja CREAMi outer bowl and install the Creamerizer Paddle onto the outer bowl lid. Secure the lid to the outer bowl.
4. Place the outer bowl assembly onto the motor base and turn the handle to the right to raise and lock the platform in position.
5. Press the GELATO button.
6. Once the program is complete, scoop the gelato

from the pint and serve immediately.

Per Serving

Calories: 456 | Fat:7g | Carbs:12g | Protein:7g | Fiber: 2g

MARSHMALLOW GELATO

Prep time: 20 minutes | Cook time: 5 minutes | Serves 4

- 1 cup whole milk
- ½ cup heavy cream
- ¼ cup granulated sugar
- 3 egg yolks
- Pinch of sea salt
- ¼ cup mini marshmallows

1. Preheat the oven to broil. Lightly grease a baking sheet.
2. Arrange the marshmallows onto the prepared baking sheet in a single layer.
3. Broil for about 5 minutes, flipping once halfway through, until golden brown.
4. Meanwhile, in a small saucepan, whisk together the milk, heavy cream, sugar, egg yolks, and a pinch of salt until well combined.
5. Place the saucepan over medium heat and cook for about 1 minute, stirring continuously, until the mixture slightly thickens.

6. Remove from the heat and stir in half of the broiled marshmallows.
7. Transfer the mixture into an empty Ninja CREAMi pint.
8. Place the pint in an ice bath to cool completely.
9. After cooling, cover the pint with the storage lid and freeze for 24 hours.
10. Reserve the remaining broiled marshmallows in the freezer.
11. After 24 hours, remove the lid from the frozen pint and place it into the Ninja CREAMi outer bowl.
12. Install the Creamerizer Paddle onto the outer bowl lid.
13. Rotate the lid clockwise to lock it onto the outer bowl.
14. Press the Power button to turn on the unit.
15. Press the GELATO button.
16. When the program is complete, use a spoon to create a 1 ½-inch wide hole

in the center of the gelato, reaching the bottom of the pint.

17. Add the reserved frozen broiled marshmallows into the hole and press the MIX-IN button.
18. When the program is complete, remove the outer bowl from the machine.
19. Transfer the gelato into serving bowls and serve immediately.

Per Serving

Calories: 250 | Fat: 17g | Carbs: 22g | Fiber: 0g | Protein: 5g

MAPLE GELATO

Prep time: 5 minutes | Cook time: 3 minutes | Serves 4

- 4 large egg yolks
- ½ cup plus 1 tablespoon light brown sugar
- 1 tablespoon maple syrup
- 1 teaspoon maple extract
- 1 cup whole milk
- ⅓ cup heavy cream

1. In a small saucepan, whisk together the egg yolks, brown sugar, maple syrup, and maple extract until well combined.
2. Add the milk and heavy cream, and whisk until well combined.
3. Place the saucepan over medium heat and cook for about 2-3 minutes, stirring continuously, until the mixture slightly thickens.
4. Remove from the heat and strain the mixture through a fine-mesh strainer into an empty Ninja CREAMi pint.
5. Place the pint in an ice bath to cool completely.
6. After cooling, cover the pint with the storage lid and freeze for 24 hours.
7. After 24 hours, remove the lid from the frozen pint and place it into the Ninja CREAMi outer bowl.
8. Install the Creamerizer Paddle onto the outer bowl lid.
9. Rotate the lid clockwise to lock it onto the outer bowl.
10. Press the Power button to turn on the unit.
11. Press the GELATO button.
12. When the program is complete, remove the outer bowl from the machine. Transfer the gelato into serving bowls and serve immediately.

Per Serving

Calories: 290 | Fat: 14g | Carbs: 19g | Fiber: 0g | Protein: 8g

SWEET POTATO GELATO

Prep time: 5 minutes | Cook time: 3 minutes | Serves 4

- ½ cup canned sweet potato puree
- 4 large egg yolks
- ¼ cup granulated sugar
- ½ teaspoon ground cinnamon
- ⅛ teaspoon ground nutmeg
- 1 cup heavy cream
- 1 teaspoon vanilla extract

1. In a small saucepan, whisk together the sweet potato puree, egg yolks, sugar, cinnamon, and nutmeg until well combined.
2. Add the heavy cream and vanilla extract, and whisk until well combined.
3. Place the saucepan over medium heat and cook for about 2-3 minutes, stirring continuously, until the mixture slightly thickens.
4. Remove from the heat and strain the mixture through a fine-mesh strainer into an empty Ninja CREAMi pint.
5. Place the pint in an ice bath to cool completely.
6. After cooling, cover the pint with the storage lid and freeze for 24 hours.
7. After 24 hours, remove the lid from the frozen pint and place it into the Ninja CREAMi outer bowl.
8. Install the Creamerizer Paddle onto the outer bowl lid.
9. Rotate the lid clockwise to lock it onto the outer bowl.
10. Press the Power button to turn on the unit.
11. Press the GELATO button.
12. When the program is complete, remove the outer bowl from the machine.
13. Transfer the gelato into serving bowls and serve immediately.

Per Serving

Calories: 310 | Fat: 24g | Carbs: 22g | Fiber: 3g | Protein: 9g

TIRAMISU GELATO

Prep time: 15 minutes | Cook time: 6 minutes | Serves 4

- 4 large egg yolks
- ⅓ cup granulated sugar
- 1 cup whole milk
- ⅓ cup heavy (whipping) cream

- ¼ cup cream cheese
- 1 tablespoon instant coffee
- 1 teaspoon rum extract
- ¼ cup ladyfinger pieces

1. Fill a large bowl with ice water and set it aside.
2. In a small saucepan, whisk together the egg yolks and sugar until the mixture is fully combined and the sugar is dissolved. Do not do this over heat.
3. Whisk in the milk, heavy cream, cream cheese, instant coffee, and rum extract.
4. Place the pan over medium heat. Cook, stirring constantly with a rubber spatula, until the temperature reaches 165°F to 175°F on an instant-read thermometer.
5. Remove the pan from the heat and pour the base through a fine-mesh strainer into a clean Ninja CREAMi pint. Carefully place the pint in the prepared ice water bath, ensuring the water does not spill into the base.
6. Once the base has cooled, place the storage lid on the pint and freeze for 24 hours.
7. Remove the pint from the freezer and take off the lid. Place the pint in the Ninja CREAMi outer bowl, install the Creamerizer Paddle in the outer bowl lid, and lock the lid assembly onto the outer bowl. Place the bowl assembly on the motor base, and twist the handle to the right to raise the platform and lock it in place. Select the GELATO function.
8. Once the machine has finished processing, remove the lid from the pint. Use a spoon to create a 1 ½-inch wide hole that reaches the bottom of the pint. It is okay if the mixture reaches above the Max Fill line during this process. Add the ladyfinger pieces to the hole in the pint, replace the lid, and select the MIX-IN function.
9. Once the machine has finished processing, remove the gelato from the pint. Serve immediately.

Per Serving

Calories: 250 | Fat: 18g | Carbs: 18g | Fiber: 0g | Protein: 8g

HONEY PEACH GELATO

Prep time: 5 minutes | Cook time: 35 minutes | Serves 4-6

- ½ cup heavy cream
- 2 cups milk
- ¾ cup granulated sugar
- 1 cup sliced peaches
- 1 tablespoon vanilla extract
- ¼ cup honey

1. In a blender, combine the heavy cream, whole milk, granulated sugar, sliced peaches, vanilla extract, and honey. Blend until completely smooth.
2. Pour the blended mixture into a Ninja CREAMi pint container. Secure the lid.
3. Freeze the pint container for at least 24 hours.
4. After 24 hours, remove the lid and place the frozen pint container into the Ninja CREAMi outer bowl. Install the Creamerizer Paddle into the outer bowl lid.
5. Lock the lid by rotating it clockwise.
6. Turn the Ninja CREAMi on, and press the "GELATO" button.
7. If the gelato is not smooth enough after the initial cycle, use the "RE-SPIN" function as needed.
8. Scoop and serve immediately.

Per Serving

Calories: 210 | Fat: 11g | Carbs: 27g | Fiber: 2g | Protein: 8g

CARROT GELATO

Prep time: 5 minutes | Cook time: 3 minutes | Serves 4

- 3 large egg yolks
- ⅓ cup coconut sugar
- 1 tablespoon brown rice syrup
- ½ cup heavy cream
- 1 cup unsweetened almond milk
- ½ cup carrot puree
- ½ teaspoon ground cinnamon
- ¼ teaspoon ground nutmeg
- ¼ teaspoon ground ginger
- ¼ teaspoon ground cloves
- ¾ teaspoon vanilla extract

1. In a small saucepan, whisk together the egg yolks, coconut sugar, and brown rice syrup until well combined.
2. Add the heavy cream, almond milk, carrot puree, and spices, and whisk until well combined.
3. Place the saucepan over medium heat and cook for about 2-3 minutes, stirring continuously, until the mixture slightly thickens.
4. Remove from the heat and stir in the vanilla extract.
5. Strain the mixture through a fine-mesh strainer into an empty Ninja CREAMi pint.
6. Place the pint in an ice bath to cool completely.
7. After cooling, cover the pint with the storage lid and freeze for 24 hours.
8. After 24 hours, remove the lid from the frozen pint and place it into the Ninja CREAMi outer bowl.
9. Install the Creamerizer Paddle onto the outer bowl lid.
10. Rotate the lid clockwise to lock it onto the outer bowl.
11. Press the Power button to turn on the unit.
12. Press the GELATO button.
13. When the program is complete, remove the outer bowl from the machine.
14. Transfer the gelato into serving bowls and serve immediately.

Per Serving

Calories: 210 | Fat: 15g | Carbs: 19g | Fiber: 2g | Protein: 6g

DOUBLE DARK CHOCOLATE GELATO

Prep time: 5 minutes | Cook time: 35 minutes | Serves 4-6

- 1 ½ cups heavy cream
- 2 cups whole milk
- ¾ cup granulated sugar
- ¼ teaspoon salt
- 7 ounces high-quality dark chocolate (chopped)
- 1 teaspoon vanilla extract

1. In a medium saucepan, combine the heavy cream, milk, sugar, and salt. Heat over medium heat, stirring occasionally, until the sugar and salt are dissolved. Do not boil.
2. Remove the saucepan from the heat. Add the chopped dark chocolate and stir until completely melted and smooth.
3. Stir in the vanilla extract.
4. Pour the chocolate mixture through a fine-mesh strainer into an empty Ninja CREAMi pint.
5. Place the pint in an ice bath to cool completely.
6. Once cooled, cover the pint with the storage lid and freeze for 24 hours.
7. After 24 hours, remove the lid from the frozen pint and place it into the Ninja CREAMi outer bowl.
8. Install the Creamerizer Paddle onto the outer bowl lid.
9. Rotate the lid clockwise to lock it onto the outer bowl.
10. Press the Power button to turn on the unit.
11. Press the GELATO button.
12. When the program is complete, if the texture is not smooth, process again on the RESPIN setting.
13. Remove the outer bowl from the machine. Transfer the gelato into serving bowls and serve immediately.

Per Serving

Calories: 380 | Fat: 30g | Carbs: 27g | Fiber: 4g | Protein: 5g

BLUEBERRY VANILLA PROTEIN SORBET

Prep time: 10 minutes | Cook time: 15 minutes | Serves 4

- 1 cup vanilla almond milk
- 3 tablespoons honey
- 1 (12-ounce) bag frozen blueberries
- 1 scoop vanilla protein powder

1. In a bowl, mix the vanilla almond milk, honey, and protein powder until fully combined.
2. Add the frozen blueberries to an empty Ninja CREAMi pint and pour the almond milk mixture over them.
3. Cover with a storage lid and freeze for 24 hours.
4. After freezing, remove the lid and place the pint into the Ninja CREAMi outer bowl.
5. Install the Creamerizer Paddle onto the outer bowl lid.
6. Rotate the lid clockwise to lock it in place.
7. Press the Power button to turn on the unit.
8. Select the GELATO function.
9. Once the cycle is complete, remove the outer bowl and remove the sorbet.
10. Serve immediately in bowls and enjoy.

Per Serving

Calories: 230 | Fat: 1.5g | Carbs: 50.9g | Fiber: 8.7g | Protein: 9.5g

CHAPTER 4: SORBET RECIPES

PASSIONFRUIT PEACH SORBET

Prep time: 10 minutes | Cook time: 15 minutes | Serves 4

- 1 cup passionfruit seltzer
- 3 tablespoons agave nectar
- 1 (15¼-ounce) can peaches in heavy syrup, drained

1. In a medium bowl, combine the passionfruit seltzer and agave nectar. Whisk until the agave nectar is completely dissolved.
2. Place the drained peaches into a Ninja CREAMi pint container. Pour the seltzer mixture over the peaches.
3. Secure the lid on the pint container and freeze for 24 hours.
4. After 24 hours, remove the lid from the frozen pint.
5. Install the Creamerizer Paddle onto the outer bowl lid.
6. Place the frozen pint into the outer bowl and lock the lid into place on the Ninja CREAMi machine.
7. Press the Power button to turn on the machine.
8. Press the Sorbet button to start the processing cycle.
9. Once the cycle is complete, remove the outer bowl from the machine.
10. Scoop the sorbet into serving bowls and serve immediately.

Per Serving

Calories: **271** | Fat: **1.5g** | Carbs: **65.4g** | Fiber: **9.5g** | Protein: **5.3g**

ITALIAN ICE SORBET

Prep time: 3 minutes | Cook time: 5 minutes | Serves 1

- 12 fluid ounces lemonade
- Sweetener (optional, to taste)
- If using a tart lemonade, substitute 6 fluid ounces of water for 6 fluid ounces of the lemonade.

1. Pour the lemonade (or lemonade and water mixture) into a Ninja CREAMi pint container. Freeze on a level surface in your freezer for 24 hours.
2. After 24 hours, remove the frozen pint from the freezer and remove the lid.
3. Place the frozen pint into the outer bowl. Install the Creamerizer Paddle onto the outer bowl lid. Place the outer bowl into the Ninja CREAMi machine and lock it into place.
4. Press the Sorbet button to start the processing cycle.
5. Once the cycle is complete, remove the outer bowl from the machine.
6. Scoop and serve immediately.

Per Serving

Calories: **236** | Protein: **8g** | Carbs: **58g** | Fiber: **0.5g** | Fat: **14g**

STRAWBERRY KIWI SORBET

Prep time: 5 minutes | Cook time: 5 minutes | Serves 4

- 2 cups sliced strawberries
- 4 sliced kiwis
- ⅛ cup raw agave
- ¼ cup water

1. Add all ingredients to a blender.
2. Blend until smooth.
3. Pour the mixture into a Ninja CREAMi pint container.
4. Freeze for 24 hours.
5. Place the frozen pint into the outer bowl. Install the Creamerizer Paddle onto the outer bowl lid. Place the outer bowl into the Ninja CREAMi machine and lock it into place.
6. Press the Sorbet button to start the processing cycle.
7. Scoop and serve immediately.

Per Serving

Calories: 206 | Protein: 9.8 | Fat: 15.36 | Carbs: 7.92 | Fiber: 4g

RED VELVET SORBET

Prep time: 35 minutes | Cook time: 10 minutes | Serves 2

- 4 large egg yolks
- 2 tablespoons cocoa powder
- ¼ cup granulated sugar
- 1 cup milk
- ¼ cup cream cheese, softened
- ⅓ cup heavy cream
- 1 teaspoon red food coloring
- 1 teaspoon vanilla extract

1. In a medium bowl, whisk together the egg yolks, cocoa powder, and granulated sugar until well combined.
2. Stir in the milk, softened cream cheese, heavy cream, red food coloring, and vanilla extract. Whisk until smooth.
3. Pour the mixture into a medium saucepan over medium heat.
4. Cook, stirring constantly, until the mixture reaches 165°F (74°C) on a candy thermometer.
5. Remove from heat and let cool for 20 minutes.
6. Transfer the cooled mixture into a Ninja CREAMi pint container.
7. Freeze for 24 hours.
8. Place the frozen pint into the outer bowl. Install the Creamerizer Paddle onto the outer bowl lid. Place the outer bowl into the Ninja CREAMi machine and lock it into place.
9. Press the Sorbet button to start the processing cycle.
10. Scoop and serve immediately.

Per Serving

Calories: 410 | Protein: 12.77 | Fat: 29.63 | Carbs: 25.16 | Fiber: 1g

PEACH-SELTZER SORBET

Prep time: 10 minutes | Cook time: 10 minutes | Serves 4

- 3 tablespoons agave nectar
- 1 cup passionfruit seltzer
- 1 (15.25-ounce) can peaches in heavy syrup, drained

1. In a medium bowl, combine the passionfruit seltzer and agave nectar. Whisk until the agave nectar is completely dissolved.
2. Place the drained peaches into a Ninja CREAMi pint container. Pour the seltzer mixture over the peaches. Secure the lid on the pint container.
3. Freeze the pint for 24 hours.
4. After 24 hours, remove the lid from the frozen pint. place the pint into the outer bowl. Install the Creamerizer Paddle onto the outer bowl lid. Place the outer bowl into the Ninja CREAMi machine and lock it into place.
5. Press the Power button to turn on the machine, and then press the Sorbet button to start the processing cycle.

6. Scoop the sorbet from the pint and serve chilled.

Per Serving

Calories: 271 | Fat: 1.5g |Carbs: 65.4g | Fiber: 9.5g | Protein: 5.3g

STRAWBERRY AND CHAMPAGNE DELISH SORBET

Prep Time: 10 minutes | Cook time: 15 minutes | Serves 2

- 1 (2-ounce) packet strawberry-flavored gelatin
- ¾ cup boiling water
- ½ cup light corn syrup
- 3 fluid ounces champagne
- 1 large egg white, lightly beaten

1. In a bowl, dissolve the gelatin in the boiling water. Whisk in the corn syrup, champagne, and lightly beaten egg white.
2. Pour the mixture into a Ninja CREAMi pint container. Freeze on a level surface in your freezer for 24 hours.
3. After 24 hours, remove the frozen pint from the freezer and remove the lid.
4. Place the frozen pint into the outer bowl. Install the Creamerizer Paddle onto the outer bowl lid. Place the outer bowl into the Ninja CREAMi machine and lock it into place.
5. Press the Sorbet button to start the processing cycle.
6. Once the cycle is complete, remove the outer bowl from the machine.

7. Scoop and serve immediately.

Per Serving

Calories: 494 | Fat:14g | Carbs:3g | Protein:12g | Fiber: 0g

BLUEBERRY LEMON SORBET

Prep time: 5 minutes | Cook time: 5 minutes | Serves 1

- 1 tablespoon cream cheese, softened
- ¼ cup milk
- 1 ½ cups lemonade
- ⅓ cup blueberries (fresh or frozen)

1. In a medium mixing bowl, whisk together the softened cream cheese and milk until mostly smooth. Small lumps of cream cheese are acceptable.
2. Add the lemonade and stir thoroughly.
3. Pour the mixture into a Ninja CREAMi pint container, add the blueberries, and freeze on a level surface in your freezer for 24 hours.
4. After 24 hours, remove the frozen pint from the freezer and remove the lid.
5. Place the frozen pint into the outer bowl. Install the Creamerizer Paddle onto the outer bowl lid. Place the outer bowl into the Ninja CREAMi machine and lock it into place.
6. Press the Sorbet button to start the processing cycle.
7. Once the cycle is complete, remove the outer bowl from the machine.
8. If the sorbet is not creamy enough, place the outer bowl back into the Ninja CREAMi machine and lock it into place. Press the Re-spin button. Remove the outer bowl after the Re-spin cycle is complete.
9. Scoop and serve immediately.

Per Serving

Calories: 160 | Fat: 5g | Carbs: 30g | Fiber: 2g | Protein: 6g

HEARTY BANANA SORBET

Prep Time: 10 minutes | Cook time: 10 minutes | Serves 2

- 1 frozen banana
- 1 teaspoon cold water
- 2 teaspoons caramel sauce

1. Place the frozen banana, cold water, and caramel sauce in a Ninja CREAMi pint container and freeze for 24 hours on a level surface in your freezer.
2. After 24 hours, remove the frozen pint from the freezer and remove the lid.
3. Place the frozen pint into the outer bowl. Install the Creamerizer Paddle onto the outer bowl lid. Place the outer bowl into the Ninja CREAMi machine and lock it into place.
4. Press the Sorbet button to start the processing cycle.
5. Once the cycle is complete, remove the outer bowl from the machine.
6. Scoop and serve immediately.

Per Serving

Calories: 261 | Fat:8g | Carbs:13g | Protein:9g | Fiber: 3g

LUSCIOUS LAVENDER SOUR CHERRY SORBET

Prep time: 5 minutes | Cook time: 35 minutes | Serves 6

- 3 cups pitted, sliced sour cherries (frozen recommended for best results)
- ½ teaspoon dried lavender
- ¾ cup granulated sugar
- ½ teaspoon salt
- 2 tablespoons vanilla extract
- 2 ½ teaspoons lime juice
- ¼ cup water (if needed for blending)

1. In a high-speed blender, combine the frozen sour cherries, lavender, sugar, salt, vanilla extract, and lime juice.
2. Blend until very smooth. If the mixture is too thick to blend smoothly, add the ¼ cup of water, a tablespoon at a time, until the mixture blends.
3. Pour the blended mixture into a Ninja CREAMi pint container.
4. Secure the lid and freeze for at least 24 hours.
5. After 24 hours, remove the frozen pint from the freezer and remove the lid.
6. Place the frozen pint into the outer bowl. Install the Creamerizer Paddle onto the outer bowl lid. Place the outer bowl into the Ninja CREAMi machine and lock it into place.
7. Press the Sorbet button to start the processing cycle.
8. If the sorbet is still crumbly or not smooth enough after the first cycle, remove the outer bowl, and then place it back into the Ninja CREAMi.
9. Press the Re-spin button.
10. Repeat the re-spin process if needed.
11. Once the desired consistency is achieved, scoop the sorbet into serving bowls and serve immediately.

Per Serving

Calories: 120 | Fat: 0g | Carbs: 31g | Fiber: 3g | Protein: 5g

MIXED BERRY PROTEIN SORBET

Prep time: 10 minutes | Cook time: 15 minutes | Serves 4

- 1 cup mixed berry seltzer
- 3 tablespoons honey
- 1 (12-ounce) bag frozen mixed berries
- 1 scoop vanilla protein powder

1. In a medium bowl, whisk together the seltzer, honey, and protein powder until fully combined.
2. Place the frozen mixed berries into a Ninja CREAMi pint container and pour the seltzer mixture over them.
3. Secure the lid and freeze for 24 hours.
4. After 24 hours, remove the lid from the frozen pint.
5. Place the frozen pint into the outer bowl. Install the Creamerizer Paddle onto the outer bowl lid. Place the outer bowl into the Ninja CREAMi machine and lock it into place.
6. Press the Power button.
7. Press the Sorbet button.
8. Once the cycle is complete, remove the outer bowl from the machine.
9. Scoop and serve immediately.

Per Serving

Calories: 252 | Fat: 1.2g | Carbs: 55.8g | Fiber: 10.4g | Protein: 9.6g

MANGO COCONUT PROTEIN SORBET

Prep time: 10 minutes | Cook time: 15 minutes | Serves 4

- 1 cup coconut water
- 3 tablespoons maple syrup
- 1 (16-ounce) bag frozen mango chunks
- 1 scoop unflavored protein powder

1. In a medium bowl, whisk together the coconut water, maple syrup, and protein powder until well blended.
2. Add the frozen mango chunks to a Ninja CREAMi pint container and pour the coconut mixture over them.
3. Secure the lid and freeze for 24 hours.
4. After 24 hours, remove the lid.
5. Place the frozen pint into the outer bowl. Install the Creamerizer Paddle onto the outer bowl lid. Place the outer bowl into the Ninja CREAMi machine and lock it into place.
6. Press the Power button.
7. Press the Sorbet button.
8. Once the cycle is complete, remove the outer bowl from the machine.

9. Scoop into bowls and serve immediately.

Per Serving

Calories: 235 | Fat: 0.8g | Carbs: 57.3g | Fiber: 6.2g | Protein: 7.8g

STRAWBERRY BANANA PROTEIN SORBET

Prep time: 10 minutes | Cook time: 15 minutes | Serves 4

- 1 cup almond milk
- 3 tablespoons agave nectar
- 1 (16-ounce) bag frozen strawberries
- 1 small banana, sliced
- 1 scoop strawberry or vanilla protein powder

1. In a medium bowl, whisk together the almond milk, agave nectar, and protein powder until smooth.
2. Add the frozen strawberries and banana slices to a Ninja CREAMi pint container and pour the almond milk mixture over them.
3. Secure the lid and freeze for 24 hours.
4. After 24 hours, remove the lid.
5. Place the frozen pint into the outer bowl. Install the Creamerizer Paddle onto the outer bowl lid. Place the outer bowl into the Ninja CREAMi machine and lock it into place.
6. Press the Power button.
7. Press the Sorbet button.
8. Once the cycle is complete, remove the outer bowl from the machine.

9. Scoop into bowls and serve immediately.

Per Serving

Calories: 259 | Fat: 1.3g | Carbs: 59.7g | Fiber: 7.9g | Protein: 8.2g

PINEAPPLE VANILLA PROTEIN SORBET

Prep time: 10 minutes | Cook time: 15 minutes | Serves 4

- 1 cup vanilla almond milk
- 3 tablespoons honey
- 1 (16-ounce) bag frozen pineapple chunks
- 1 scoop vanilla protein powder

1. In a medium bowl, whisk together the vanilla almond milk, honey, and protein powder until well combined.
2. Add the frozen pineapple chunks to a Ninja CREAMi pint container and pour the liquid mixture over them.
3. Secure the lid and freeze for 24 hours.
4. After 24 hours, remove the lid.
5. Place the frozen pint into the outer bowl. Install the Creamerizer Paddle onto the outer bowl lid. Place the outer bowl into the Ninja CREAMi machine and lock it into place.
6. Press the Power button.
7. Press the Sorbet button.
8. Once the cycle is complete, remove the outer bowl from the machine.
9. Scoop into bowls and serve immediately.

Per Serving

Calories: 248 | Fat: 1.1g | Carbs: 58.2g | Fiber: 6.8g | Protein: 8.7g

AVOCADO SORBET

Prep time: 10 minutes | Cook time: 10 minutes | Serves 4

- ¾ cup water
- 2 tablespoons light corn syrup
- Pinch of sea salt
- ⅔ cup granulated sugar
- 1 large ripe avocado, peeled, pitted, and chopped
- 3 fluid ounces fresh lime juice

1. In a medium saucepan, combine water, corn syrup, and sea salt. Whisk until well combined.
2. Place the saucepan over medium heat.
3. Slowly add the sugar, whisking continuously until well combined. Bring to a boil.
4. Remove the saucepan from heat and set aside to cool completely.
5. In a high-speed blender, combine the cooled sugar mixture, avocado, and lime juice. Blend until smooth.
6. Transfer the mixture into a Ninja CREAMi pint container.
7. Secure the lid and freeze for 24 hours.
8. After 24 hours, remove the lid from the frozen pint.
9. Place the frozen pint into the outer bowl. Install the Creamerizer Paddle onto the outer bowl lid. Place the outer bowl into the Ninja CREAMi machine and lock it into place.
10. Press the Power button. Press the Sorbet button.
11. Once the cycle is complete, remove the outer bowl from the machine.
12. Scoop and serve immediately.

Per Serving

Calories: 160 | Fat: 7g | Carbs: 25g | Fiber: 7g | Protein: 4g

WATERMELON LIME SORBET

Prep time: 10 minutes | Cook time: 15 minutes | Serves 4

- 1 cup lime seltzer
- 3 tablespoons agave nectar
- 3 cups cubed and frozen seedless watermelon

1. In a medium bowl, whisk the lime seltzer and agave nectar until fully combined.
2. Add the frozen watermelon cubes to a Ninja CREAMi pint container and pour the seltzer mixture over them.
3. Secure the lid and freeze for 24 hours.
4. After 24 hours, remove the lid.
5. Place the frozen pint into the outer bowl. Install the Creamerizer Paddle onto the outer bowl lid. Place the outer bowl into the Ninja CREAMi machine and lock it into place.
6. Press the Power button.
7. Press the Sorbet button.
8. Once the cycle is complete, remove the outer bowl from the machine.
9. Scoop into bowls and serve immediately.

Per Serving

Calories: 134 | Fat: 0.3g | Carbs: 34.6g | Fiber: 1.2g | Protein: 1.3g

PINEAPPLE ORANGE SORBET

Prep time: 10 minutes | Cook time: 15 minutes |Serves 4

- 1 cup orange seltzer
- 3 tablespoons honey
- 1 (16-ounce) bag frozen pineapple chunks

1. In a medium bowl, whisk the orange seltzer and honey until the honey is dissolved.
2. Add the frozen pineapple chunks to a Ninja CREAMi pint container and pour the seltzer mixture over them.
3. Secure the lid and freeze for 24 hours.
4. After 24 hours, remove the lid.
5. Place the frozen pint into the outer bowl. Install the Creamerizer Paddle onto the outer bowl lid. Place the outer bowl into the Ninja CREAMi machine and lock it into place.
6. Press the Power button.
7. Press the Sorbet button.
8. Once the cycle is complete, remove the outer bowl from the machine.
9. Scoop into bowls and serve immediately.

Per Serving

Calories: 158 | Fat: 0.2g | Carbs: 41.2g | Fiber: 2.6g | Protein: 1.6g

CHAPTER 5: SMOOTHIE BOWLS RECIPES

FROZEN OATMEAL SMOOTHIE BOWL

Prep time: 10 minutes | Cook time: 10 minutes | Serves 2

- ¼ cup quick oats
- 1 cup vanilla whole milk yogurt
- ½ cup banana, chopped
- 1 tablespoon honey

1. Microwave ½ cup of water and the oats in a small bowl for 1 minute or until the oats are soft.
2. Stir in the yogurt, banana, and honey until everything is well combined.
3. Transfer the mixture into an empty Ninja CREAMi Pint.
4. Cover the pint with the lid and freeze for 24 hours.
5. After 24 hours, remove the lid and place the pint into the outer bowl of the Ninja CREAMi.
6. Install the Creamerizer Paddle onto the lid of the outer bowl, then rotate the lid clockwise to lock.
7. Turn the unit on.
8. Press the SMOOTHIE button.
9. When the program is complete, turn the outer bowl and release it from the machine.
10. Transfer the smoothie into serving bowls and serve with your favorite toppings.

Per Serving

Calories: 340 | Fat: 6g | Carbs: 56g | Fiber: 11g | Protein: 20g

COFFEE SMOOTHIE BOWL

Prep time: 5 minutes | Cook time: 5 minutes | Serves 1

Smoothie Bowl:

- 1 cup coffee (brewed; not just the coffee beans or grounds)
- ½ cup oat milk
- 2 tablespoons mocha almond butter
- 1 cup raspberries
- 1 banana

Toppings:

- 1 banana, sliced
- ½ cup raspberries
- 1 tablespoon sliced almonds
- ¼ cup chocolate-covered espresso beans
- 1 teaspoon honey or maple syrup

1. Combine all smoothie bowl ingredients in a blender and blend until smooth.
2. Pour into an empty Ninja CREAMi Pint container and freeze for 24 hours.
3. After 24 hours, remove the Pint from the freezer. Remove the lid.
4. Place the Ninja CREAMi Pint into the outer bowl. Place the outer bowl with the Pint in it into the Ninja CREAMi machine and turn until the outer bowl locks into place. Push the SMOOTHIE BOWL button. During the SMOOTHIE function, the ingredients will mix together and become very creamy.
5. Once the SMOOTHIE BOWL function has ended, turn the outer bowl and release it from the Ninja CREAMi machine.
6. Scoop the smoothie into a bowl. Drizzle with maple syrup or honey. Top with sliced almonds, chocolate-covered espresso beans, raspberries, and sliced bananas.
7. Your smoothie bowl is ready to eat!

Per Serving

Calories: 906 | Protein: 20g | Carbs: 128g | Fiber: 9g | Fat: 41g

FRUITY GINGER SMOOTHIE BOWL

Prep time: 10 minutes | Cook time: 10 minutes | Serves 1

- 1 ripe banana
- 1 teaspoon fresh ginger, minced
- ½ teaspoon vanilla extract
- 1 cup strawberries
- ½ teaspoon cinnamon
- ½ cup unsweetened almond milk

1. In a blender, combine all the ingredients and blend until smooth.
2. Pour this mixture up to the MAX FILL line of a Ninja CREAMi pint.
3. Secure the lid on the pint and freeze for 24 hours.
4. After 24 hours, remove the lid, place the pint into the outer bowl of the Ninja CREAMi, and install the Creamerizer Paddle.
5. Secure the lid, press the Power Button, and select the SMOOTHIE function.
6. Scoop the smoothie from the pint and serve as desired.

Per Serving

Calories: 396 | Fat: 13g | Carbs: 69g | Fiber: 15g | Protein: 8g

LEAN GREEN SMOOTHIE

Prep time: 5 minutes | Cook time: 3 minutes | Serves 4

- 2 cups frozen pineapple chunks
- 2 cups frozen mango chunks
- 2 handfuls baby spinach
- 1 scoop vanilla protein powder
- 1 cup orange juice
- ¼ cup water (or more, if needed for blending)

1. In a high-speed blender, combine the frozen pineapple, frozen mango, baby spinach, vanilla protein powder, and orange juice.
2. Add the water, a little at a time, until you achieve a thick, smooth consistency. It should be pourable but not too thin.
3. Pour the blended mixture into a Ninja CREAMi pint container.
4. Secure the lid and freeze for at least 24 hours.
5. After 24 hours, remove the frozen pint from the freezer and remove the lid.
6. Place the frozen pint into the outer bowl. Install the Creamerizer Paddle onto the outer bowl lid. Place the outer bowl into the Ninja CREAMi machine and lock it into place.
7. Press the "Sorbet" button to start the processing cycle.
8. If the frozen dessert is still crumbly or not smooth enough after the first cycle, remove the outer bowl, place it back into the Ninja CREAMi, and press the "Re-spin" button.
9. Repeat the re-spin process if needed to reach desired creamy consistency.
10. Scoop the frozen dessert into bowls and serve immediately.

Per Serving

Calories: 158 | Fat: 0.9 g | Carbs: 31.5 g | Protein: 6.4 g | Fiber: 5g

RASPBERRY AND SOY MILK SMOOTHIE BOWL

Prep time: 10 minutes | Cook time: 10 minutes |Serves 1

- ½ cup raspberries
- 2 bananas, frozen
- 1½ cups soy milk
- 3 teaspoons honey
- 2 teaspoons almond butter

1. Blend the raspberries with bananas, soy milk, honey, and almond butter in a blender until smooth.
2. Pour this mixture up to the MAX FILL line of a Ninja CREAMi pint.
3. Secure the lid on the pint and freeze for 24 hours.
4. After 24 hours, remove the lid, place the pint into the outer bowl of the Ninja CREAMi, and install the Creamerizer Paddle.
5. Secure the lid, press the Power Button, and select the SMOOTHIE function.
6. Scoop the smoothie from the pint and serve as desired.

Per Serving

Calories: 700 | Fat: 25g | Carbs: 90g | Fiber: 15g | Protein: 22g

MIXED BERRIES SMOOTHIE BOWL

Prep time: 10 minutes | Cook time: 15 minutes |Serves 4

- ¾ cup fresh strawberries, hulled and quartered
- ¾ cup fresh raspberries
- ¾ cup fresh blueberries
- ¾ cup fresh blackberries
- ¼ cup plain Greek yogurt
- 1 tablespoon honey

1. In an empty Ninja CREAMi pint container, place the berries and with the back of a spoon, firmly press the berries below the Max Fill line.
2. Add the yogurt and honey and stir to combine.
3. Cover the container with the storage lid and freeze for 24 hours.
4. After 24 hours, remove the lid from the container and place it into the Outer Bowl of the Ninja CREAMi.
5. Install the Creamerizer Paddle onto the lid of the Outer Bowl.
6. Rotate the lid clockwise to lock.
7. Press the Power button to turn on the unit.
8. Press the Smoothie button.
9. When the program is completed, turn the Outer Bowl and release it from the machine.
10. Transfer the smoothie into serving bowls and serve immediately.

Per Serving

Calories: 104 | Fat: 0.5g | Carbs: 18.7g | Fiber: 4.1g | Protein: 8.6g

HEALTHY AVOCADO SMOOTHIE

Prep Time: 10 minutes | **Cook time:** 5 minutes | **Serves** 2

- 8 ice cubes
- ½ cup vanilla yogurt
- 1 ripe avocado, pitted
- 3 tablespoons honey
- 1 cup milk

1. Combine the avocado, milk, yogurt, honey, and ice cubes in an empty Ninja CREAMi pint.
2. Place the Ninja CREAMi pint in the outer bowl. Insert the outer bowl containing the pint into the Ninja CREAMi machine and turn until the outer bowl is locked into place. Select the SMOOTHIE button.
3. The ingredients will combine and become very creamy during the SMOOTHIE function.
4. Once the SMOOTHIE function has concluded, turn the outer bowl and remove it from the Ninja CREAMi machine.
5. Pour the smoothie into glasses and serve immediately.

Per Serving

Calories: 330 | **Fat:** 20g | **Carbs:** 39g | **Fiber:** 7g | **Protein:** 6g

DRAGON FRUIT SMOOTHIE

Prep time: 10 minutes | **Cook time:** 10 minutes | **Serves** 2

- 1 cup plain Greek yogurt
- 2 cups dragon fruit cubes, frozen
- 1 medium banana, frozen

1. Blend the dragon fruit with banana and yogurt in a blender until smooth.
2. Pour this mixture up to the MAX FILL line of a Ninja CREAMi pint.
3. Secure the lid on the pint and freeze for 24 hours.
4. After 24 hours, remove the lid, place the pint into the outer bowl of the Ninja CREAMi, and install the Creamerizer Paddle.
5. Secure the lid, press the Power Button, and select the SMOOTHIE function.
6. Scoop the smoothie from the pint and serve as desired.

Per Serving

Calories: 255 | **Fat:** 4g | **Carbs:** 38g | **Fiber:** 4g | **Protein:** 11g

PEAR SMOOTHIE BOWL

Prep time: 10 minutes | Cook time: 10 minutes | Serves 3

- 2 cups fresh pear, chopped
- ½ cup apple cider
- 2 tablespoons protein powder
- ¼ cup pecans
- 1 cup ice
- ½ cup Greek yogurt
- 2 cups milk

1. Blend the pear with the remaining ingredients in a blender until smooth.
2. Pour this mixture up to the MAX FILL line of a Ninja CREAMi pint.
3. Secure the lid on the pint and freeze for 24 hours.
4. After 24 hours, remove the lid, place the pint into the outer bowl of the Ninja CREAMi, and install the Creamerizer Paddle.
5. Secure the lid, press the Power Button, and select the SMOOTHIE function.
6. Scoop the smoothie from the pint and serve as desired.

Per Serving

Calories: 327 | Fat: 12g | Carbs: 38g | Fiber: 5g | Protein: 20g

STRAWBERRY-ORANGE CREME SMOOTHIE

Prep time: 5 minutes | Cook time: 5 minutes | Serves 1

- 1 (5.3 ounces) container Yoplait Greek 100 orange creme yogurt
- ½ cup fresh strawberries, hulled
- ¼ cup ice cubes (optional)
- ¼ cup orange juice

1. Place all the ingredients into an empty Ninja CREAMi Pint.
2. Place the Ninja CREAMi Pint into the outer bowl. Place the outer bowl with the Pint in it into the Ninja CREAMi machine and turn until the outer bowl locks into place. Press the SMOOTHIE button. During the SMOOTHIE function, the ingredients will mix together and become very creamy.
3. Once the SMOOTHIE function has ended, turn the outer bowl and release it from the Ninja CREAMi machine.
4. Pour the smoothie into a tall glass and serve immediately.

Per Serving

Calories: 136 | Protein: 12g | Carbs: 20g | Fiber: 1.5g | Fat: 0.3g

MATCHA GREEN TEA SMOOTHIE

Prep time: 5 minutes | **Cook time: 3 minutes** | **Serves 2**

- 2 bananas, frozen
- 2 teaspoons matcha powder
- 1 avocado, pitted and cubed
- 1 cup kale, chopped
- 1 cup almond milk (or more, if needed for blending)
- Water or ice (optional, for desired consistency)

1. In a high-speed blender, combine all ingredients (frozen bananas, matcha powder, avocado, kale, and almond milk).
2. Blend until smooth. If the mixture is too thick, add more almond milk or water, a little at a time, until you reach your desired consistency. You may also add ice to reach a colder temperature.
3. If you want an extra-smooth and chilled smoothie, pour the blended mixture into a Ninja CREAMi pint container.
4. Place the pint in the outer bowl. Install the blender blade lid. Place the outer bowl into the Ninja CREAMi machine and lock it into place.
5. Press the Smoothie button.
6. Serve immediately.

Per Serving

Calories: 270 | **Fat: 15g** | **Carbs: 35g** | **Fiber: 9g** | **Protein: 4g**

CREAMY MANGO BANANA SMOOTHIE BOWL

Prep time: 10 minutes | **Cook time: 10 minutes** | **Serves 2**

- 1 cup banana, frozen
- 3 cups mango, frozen
- ½ cup almond milk
- 2 tablespoons maple syrup

For Topping:
- 4 tablespoons granola
- 2 tablespoons passion fruit seeds

1. In a blender, combine all the ingredients except for toppings and blend until smooth.
2. Pour this mixture up to the MAX FILL line of a Ninja CREAMi pint.
3. Secure the lid on the pint and freeze for 24 hours.
4. After 24 hours, remove the lid, place the pint into the outer bowl of the Ninja CREAMi, and install the Creamerizer Paddle.
5. Secure the lid, press the Power Button, and select the SMOOTHIE function.
6. Scoop the smoothie from the pint, top with granola and passion fruit seeds, and serve as desired.

Per Serving

Calories: 423 | **Fat: 7g** | **Carbs: 94g** | **Fiber: 11g** | **Protein: 6g**

MAGICAL ENERGY ELIXIR SMOOTHIE

Prep Time: 10 minutes | Cook time: 5 minutes | Serves 2

- ½ cup frozen red grapes
- ½ cup spring greens
- ½ cup frozen bananas
- ½ frozen pear, cored and chopped
- 2 tablespoons walnuts
- Water as needed

1. Layer the spring greens, red grapes, banana, pear, walnuts, and enough water to cover the mixture in an empty Ninja CREAMi Pint.
2. Place the Ninja CREAMi Pint into the outer bowl.

Place the outer bowl with the Pint into the Ninja CREAMi machine and turn until the outer bowl locks into place. Press the SMOOTHIE button. During the SMOOTHIE function, the ingredients will mix together and become very creamy.

3. Once the SMOOTHIE function has ended, turn the outer bowl and release it from the Ninja CREAMi machine.
4. Pour the smoothie into glasses and serve immediately.

Per Serving

Calories: 190 | Fat: 10g | Carbs: 30g | Fiber: 6g | Protein: 10g

GREEN MATCHA MINT SMOOTHIE

Prep time: 5 minutes | Cook time:5 minutes |Serves 2

Smoothie:

- ⅓ cup soaked raw cashews
- 3 cups loose-packed greens (e.g., spinach, kale)
- 3 bananas, frozen
- 3 sprigs of mint leaves
- 3 teaspoons matcha powder
- 1 teaspoon vanilla powder
- 2 scoops vanilla protein powder
- 3 ½ cups unsweetened almond milk
- 1 tablespoon cacao nibs
- Maple syrup, to taste

Toppings:

- 1 tablespoon coconut flakes
- 1 tablespoon hemp seeds or sesame seeds
- 1 tablespoon cacao nibs
- 2 tablespoons puffed quinoa
- Few sprigs of mint

1. In a high-speed blender, combine all smoothie ingredients except cacao nibs.
2. Blend until a smooth consistency is achieved.
3. Add the cacao nibs and pulse briefly to break them up.
4. If you desire an even smoother and colder smoothie, pour the blended mixture into a Ninja CREAMi pint container.
5. Place the pint in the outer bowl. Install the blender blade lid. Place the outer bowl into the Ninja CREAMi machine and lock it into place.
6. Press the Smoothie button.
7. Pour into a bowl.
8. Top with your choice of toppings (coconut flakes, hemp seeds, cacao nibs, puffed quinoa, mint).
9. Add maple syrup to taste, if desired.

Per Serving

Calories: 380 | Fat: 17g | Carbs: 47g | Fiber: 10g | Protein: 15g

OAT BANANA SMOOTHIE BOWL

Prep time: 10 minutes | Cook time: 15 minutes | Serves 2

- ¼ cup quick oats
- ½ cup water
- 1 cup vanilla Greek yogurt
- 3 tablespoons honey
- ½ cup banana, peeled and sliced

1. Combine the water and oats in a microwave-safe bowl and microwave for 1 minute on High.
2. After removing from the microwave, add the yogurt, banana, and honey and stir until well combined.
3. Pour this mixture up to the MAX FILL line of a Ninja CREAMi pint.
4. Secure the lid on the pint and freeze for 24 hours.
5. After 24 hours, remove the lid, place the pint into the outer bowl of the Ninja CREAMi, and install the Creamerizer Paddle.
6. Secure the lid, press the Power Button, and select the SMOOTHIE function.
7. Scoop the smoothie from the pint and serve as desired.

Per Serving

Calories: 278 | Fat: 2.7g | Carbs: 55.7g | Fiber: 2.1g | Protein: 10.9g

BLUEBERRY CACAO SMOOTHIE

Prep time: 5 minutes | Cook time:5 minutes |Serves 2

Smoothie:

- 1 ¼ cups unsweetened vanilla almond milk
- 1 cup frozen blueberries
- 1 cup frozen spinach
- 1 tablespoon cacao powder
- 1 tablespoon hemp seeds
- 2 Medjool dates, pitted
- 1 scoop vanilla brown rice protein
- A few drops of vanilla extract

Toppings:

- 1 tablespoon coconut flakes
- 2 tablespoons cacao nibs
- 2 tablespoons goji berries
- 2 tablespoons blueberries
- 1 granola bar, crumbled

1. Blend all smoothie ingredients until a smooth, creamy puree is formed.
2. If you desire an even smoother and colder smoothie, pour the blended mixture into a Ninja CREAMi pint container.
3. Place the pint in the outer bowl. Install the blender blade lid. Place the outer bowl into the Ninja CREAMi machine and lock it into place.
4. Press the Smoothie button.
5. Pour into a bowl.
6. Top with your choice of toppings (coconut flakes, cacao nibs, goji berries, blueberries, crumbled granola bar).

Per Serving

Calories: 320 | Fat: 16g | Carbs: 40g | Fiber: 9g | Protein: 12g

CHAPTER 6:
MILKSHAKE RECIPES

CHOCOLATE PROYO MILKSHAKE

Prep time: 2 minutes | Cook time: 10 minutes | Serves 2

- 1 cup chocolate frozen yogurt
- 1 scoop chocolate protein whey powder
- 1 cup whole milk

1. Place all the ingredients in an empty Ninja CREAMi Pint and mix well.
2. Place the pint into the outer bowl of the Ninja CREAMi.
3. Install the Creamerizer Paddle onto the lid of the outer bowl, then rotate the lid clockwise to lock.
4. Turn the unit on.
5. Press the MILKSHAKE button.
6. When the program is complete, turn the outer bowl and release it from the machine.
7. Transfer the shake into serving glasses and serve immediately.

Per Serving

Calories: 243 | Fat: 7.6g | Carbs: 28g | Fiber: 0g | Protein: 15g

BLACKBERRY BANANA MILKSHAKE WITH FLAX

Prep time: 5 minutes | Cook time: 5 minutes |Serves 2

- 1 cup frozen blackberries, plus more for garnish
- 1 large frozen banana, cut into small pieces
- 1 scoop vanilla ice cream
- 1 cup skim milk
- 1 tablespoon flaxseeds

1. Combine the frozen blackberries, frozen banana pieces, vanilla ice cream, skim milk, and flaxseeds in a Ninja CREAMi pint container, ensuring it is filled below the max fill line.
2. Secure the lid tightly on the pint container and freeze for at least 24 hours, or until completely solid.
3. After 24 hours, remove the pint container from the freezer and let it sit at room temperature for 5-10 minutes to soften slightly.
4. Place the pint container in the Ninja CREAMi outer bowl, ensuring it is properly locked in place. Install the Creamerizer paddle in the outer bowl lid, and lock the lid assembly onto the outer bowl. Place the bowl assembly on the motor base and twist the handle to the right to secure it in position.
5. Select the "Milkshake" function and press start.
6. if needed use the "Re-Spin" function until the desired creamy milkshake texture is achieved.
7. Pour into 2 serving glasses. Garnish with a few fresh blackberries and mint sprigs.
8. Serve immediately.

Per Serving

Calories: 220 | Fat: 5g | Carbs: 44g | Fiber: 6g | Protein: 6g

CHOCOLATE YOGURT MILKSHAKE

Prep time: 10 minutes | **Cook time:** 10 minutes | **Serves** 2

- 1 cup frozen chocolate yogurt
- 1 scoop chocolate whey protein powder
- 1 cup whole milk

1. In an empty Ninja CREAMi pint container, place yogurt followed by protein powder and milk.
2. Place the container into the Outer Bowl of the Ninja CREAMi.
3. Install the Creamerizer Paddle onto the lid of the Outer Bowl.
4. Rotate the lid clockwise to lock.
5. Press the Power button to turn on the unit.
6. Press the Milkshake button.
7. When the program is completed, turn the Outer Bowl and release it from the machine.
8. Transfer the shake into serving glasses and serve immediately.

Per Serving

Calories: 242 | **Fat:** 4.8g | **Carbs:** 30.7g | **Fiber:** 0.4g | **Protein:** 18.6g

STRAWBERRY PLUM AND COTTAGE CHEESE MILKSHAKE

Prep time: 5 minutes | **Cook time:** 5 minutes |**Serves** 2

- 1 cup frozen strawberries, hulled and halved
- ½ cup plum, pitted and sliced
- ½ cup cottage cheese
- 2 scoops vanilla ice cream
- 1 cup low-fat milk
- 4 ice cubes

1. Combine the frozen strawberries, plum, cottage cheese, vanilla ice cream, low-fat milk, and ice cubes in a high-speed blender.
2. Process until well-blended and smooth.
3. For an even smoother and colder milkshake, pour the blended mixture into a Ninja CREAMi pint container.
4. Place the pint in the outer bowl. Install the blender blade lid. Place the outer bowl into the Ninja CREAMi machine and lock it into place.
5. Press the Milkshake button.
6. Pour the milkshake into 2 chilled glasses.

Per Serving

Calories: 310 | **Fat:** 14g | **Carbs:** 38g | **Fiber:** 4g | **Protein:** 12g

COCONUT CASHEW MILKSHAKE

Prep time: 5 minutes | Cook time: 5 minutes | Serves 2

- 1½ cups vanilla coconut milk ice cream
- ½ cup coconut milk
- ¼ cup cashew butter

1. Put the ice cream in the Ninja CREAMi pint container.
2. Create a hole in the middle using a spoon.
3. Pour the coconut milk and add the cashew butter inside the hole.
4. Freeze for 24 hours.
5. Place the pint container into the outer bowl and lock the container in the machine.
6. Select the Milkshake setting.
7. When the program is completed, remove and serve immediately.

Per Serving

Calories: 420 | Fat: 28g | Carbs: 32g | Fiber: 4g | Protein: 6g

TAHINI CHOCOLATE OAT MILKSHAKE

Prep time: 5 minutes | Cook time: 10 minutes | Serves 1

- ½ cup oat milk
- 1½ cups chocolate ice cream
- ¼ cup tahini
- 2 tablespoons brewed coffee
- 2 orange slices (for garnish)

1. Combine the tahini, oat milk, chocolate ice cream, and coffee in a Ninja CREAMi pint container.
2. Secure the lid on the pint container and freeze for 24 hours.
3. After 24 hours, remove the lid and place the frozen pint into the outer bowl of the Ninja CREAMi.
4. Insert the Creamerizer paddle, secure the lid, and press the Power Button.
5. Select the MILKSHAKE function and allow the cycle to complete.
6. If needed, use the Re-Spin function for a smoother consistency.
7. Pour the shake into a serving glass and garnish with orange slices.

Per Serving

Calories: 432 | Fat: 34g | Carbs: 45g | Fiber: 11g | Protein: 15g

DRAGON FRUIT AND BANANA MILKSHAKE

Prep time: 5 minutes | Cook time: 5 minutes |Serves 2

- 1 medium dragon fruit, peeled and cut into small pieces
- 1 medium banana, sliced
- 2 scoops (about 4 ounces) vanilla ice cream
- 1 ½ cups skim milk
- 2 tablespoons protein powder (optional)
- Ice cubes (optional, for extra chill)

1. Combine the dragon fruit, banana, vanilla ice cream, skim milk, and protein powder (if using) in a high-speed blender.
2. Add ice cubes if desired for a colder milkshake.
3. Process until well-blended and smooth.
4. For an even smoother and colder milkshake, pour the blended mixture into a Ninja CREAMi pint container.
5. Place the pint in the outer bowl. Install the blender blade lid. Place the outer bowl into the Ninja CREAMi machine and lock it into place.
6. Press the Milkshake button.
7. Pour the milkshake into 2 chilled glasses.
8. Serve and enjoy.

Per Serving

Calories: 290 | Fat: 6g | Carbs: 51g | Fiber: 7g | Protein: 8g

BANANA STRAWBERRY AND ALMOND MILKSHAKE

Prep time: 5 minutes | Cook time: 5 minutes |Serves 2

- 1 large banana, cut into small pieces
- 1 cup strawberries, hulled and halved
- 2 scoops vanilla ice cream
- 1½ cups unsweetened almond milk
- 2 tablespoons protein powder (optional)

1. Combine all ingredients in a Ninja CREAMi pint container.
2. Secure the lid and freeze for 24 hours.
3. Remove the lid and place the frozen pint into the outer bowl of the Ninja CREAMi.
4. Insert the Creamerizer paddle, secure the lid, and press the Power Button.
5. Select the MILKSHAKE function and allow the cycle to complete.
6. Use the Re-Spin function if needed for a smoother consistency.
7. Pour into 2 chilled glasses and serve immediately.

Per Serving

Calories: 290 | Fat: 7g | Carbs: 47g | Fiber: 6g | Protein: 8g

BANANA AND DATE MILKSHAKE

Prep time: 5 minutes | Cook time: 5 minutes | Serves 2

- 1 large banana, cut into small pieces
- 3 dates, pitted
- 2 scoops vanilla ice cream
- 1½ cups skim milk
- Banana slices, for garnish

1. Combine the banana, dates, vanilla ice cream, and milk in a Ninja CREAMi pint container.
2. Secure the lid and freeze for 24 hours.
3. Remove the lid and place the frozen pint into the outer bowl of the Ninja CREAMi.
4. Insert the Creamerizer paddle, secure the lid, and press the Power Button.
5. Select the MILKSHAKE function and allow the cycle to complete.
6. Use the Re-Spin function if needed for a smoother consistency.
7. Pour into 2 chilled glasses, garnish with banana slices, and serve.

Per Serving

Calories: 330 | Fat: 7g | Carbs: 64g | Fiber: 7g | Protein: 6g

PEACH GINGER AND ALMOND MILKSHAKE

Prep time: 5 minutes | Cook time: 5 minutes | Serves 2

- 1 large peach, peeled, pitted, and cut into small pieces
- ½ teaspoon ginger, freshly grated
- 1 cup unsweetened almond milk
- 1 cup frozen yogurt
- Fresh mint sprigs, for garnish

1. Combine the peach, ginger, almond milk, and frozen yogurt in a Ninja CREAMi pint container.
2. Secure the lid and freeze for 24 hours.
3. Remove the lid and place the frozen pint into the outer bowl of the Ninja CREAMi.
4. Insert the Creamerizer paddle, secure the lid, and press the Power Button.
5. Select the MILKSHAKE function and allow the cycle to complete.
6. Use the Re-Spin function if needed for a smoother consistency.
7. Pour into 2 chilled glasses, garnish with mint sprigs, and serve immediately.

Per Serving

Calories: 210 | Fat: 5g | Carbs: 36g | Fiber: 4g | Protein: 5g

PUMPKIN LATTE MILKSHAKE

Prep time: 5 minutes | Cook time: 15 minutes | Serves 4

- 2 cups whole milk
- 2 tablespoons granulated sugar
- 1 cup strong brewed coffee
- 4 cups vanilla ice cream
- ½ cup canned pumpkin puree (not pumpkin pie filling)
- 1 teaspoon pumpkin pie spice
- 2 teaspoons vanilla extract

1. In a small saucepan, heat the milk until it begins to simmer (do not boil). Remove from heat.
2. In a large bowl, combine the warm milk, pumpkin puree, sugar, pumpkin pie spice, coffee, and vanilla extract.
3. Whisk thoroughly until combined and refrigerate for 1 hour.
4. Divide the mixture between two Ninja CREAMi pint containers, adding vanilla ice cream to each.
5. Secure the lids and freeze for 24 hours.
6. After 24 hours, remove the lid from the first pint and place it into the outer bowl of the Ninja CREAMi.
7. Insert the Creamerizer paddle, secure the lid, and press the Power Button.
8. Select the MILKSHAKE function and allow the cycle to complete.
9. Use the Re-Spin function if needed for a smoother consistency.
10. Pour into serving glasses and repeat with the second pint.
11. Serve chilled, optionally topped with whipped cream and a sprinkle of pumpkin pie spice.

Per Serving

Calories: 260 | Fat: 11g | Carbs: 30g | Fiber: 1g | Protein: 6 g

BAILEYS MILKSHAKE

Prep time: 5 minutes | Cook time: 5 minutes | Serves 1

- 1 scoop vanilla ice cream
- 1 scoop chocolate ice cream
- 1 tablespoon chocolate sauce
- 1 tablespoon caramel sauce
- 2 fluid ounces Baileys Irish Cream
- 1 cup whole milk

1. Place all ingredients into an empty Ninja CREAMi pint container.
2. Place the pint container in the Ninja CREAMi outer bowl, ensuring it is properly locked in place. Install the Creamerizer paddle in the outer bowl lid, and lock the lid assembly onto the outer bowl. Place the bowl assembly on the motor base and twist the handle to the right to secure it in position.
3. Select the "Milkshake" function and press start.
4. Pour the milkshake into a serving glass and serve immediately.

Per Serving

Calories: 718 | Protein: 18g | Carbs: 85g | Fiber: 1.1g | Fat: 22g

CINNAMON DATES MILKSHAKE

Prep time: 5 minutes | Cook time: 10 minutes | Serves 2

- 3 cups milk
- 10 pitted dates
- ¼ teaspoon ground cinnamon

1. Place the milk, pitted dates, and ground cinnamon into a Ninja CREAMi pint container, ensuring it is filled below the max fill line.
2. Secure the lid tightly on the pint container and freeze for at least 24 hours, or until completely solid.
3. After 24 hours, remove the pint container from the freezer and let it sit at room temperature for 5-10 minutes to soften slightly.
4. Place the pint container in the Ninja CREAMi outer bowl, ensuring it is properly locked in place. Install the Creamerizer paddle in the outer bowl lid, and lock the lid assembly onto the outer bowl. Place the bowl assembly on the motor base and twist the handle to the right to secure it in position.
5. Select the "Milkshake" function and press start.
6. Pour the milkshake into chilled serving glasses and serve immediately.

Per Serving

Calories: 300 | Fat: 7g | Carbs: 29g | Fiber: 3g | Protein: 13g

MIXED BERRY OAT AND YOGURT MILKSHAKE

Prep time: 5 minutes | Cook time: 5 minutes | Serves 2

- 1 cup frozen mixed berries
- 1 cup frozen vanilla or plain yogurt
- ¼ cup cooked oatmeal
- 1 cup skim milk
- 2 tablespoons strawberry syrup
- Fresh mint sprigs, for garnish

1. Combine the frozen mixed berries, frozen yogurt, cooked oatmeal, skim milk, and strawberry syrup into a Ninja CREAMi pint container, ensuring it is filled below the max fill line.
2. Secure the lid tightly on the pint container and freeze for at least 24 hours, or until completely solid.
3. After 24 hours, remove the pint container from the freezer and let it sit at room temperature for 5-10 minutes to soften slightly.
4. Place the pint container in the Ninja CREAMi outer bowl, ensuring it is properly locked in place. Install the Creamerizer paddle in the outer bowl lid, and lock the lid assembly onto the outer bowl. Place the bowl assembly on the motor base and twist the handle to the right to secure it in position.
5. Select the "Milkshake" function and press start.
6. After the cycle is complete, if needed, use the "Re-Spin" function until the desired creamy milkshake texture is achieved.
7. Pour into chilled serving glasses. Garnish with a few fresh berries, a sprinkle of oats, and mint sprigs.
8. Serve immediately.

Per Serving

Calories: 240 | Fat: 4g | Carbs: 47g | Fiber: 7g | Protein: 8g

TERRIFIC VANILLA MILKSHAKE

Prep time: 10 minutes | Cook time: 10 minutes | Serves 2

- 2 cups French vanilla coffee creamer
- 1 tablespoon agave nectar
- 2 ounces vodka
- 1 tablespoon rainbow sprinkles

1. In an empty Ninja CREAMi pint container, place all ingredients and mix well.
2. Cover the container with storage lid and freeze for 24 hours.
3. After 24 hours, remove the lid from container and place it into the Outer Bowl of the Ninja CREAMi.
4. Install the Creamerizer Paddle onto the lid of the Outer Bowl.
5. Rotate the lid clockwise to lock.
6. Press the Power button to turn on the unit.
7. Press the Milkshake button.
8. When the program is completed, turn the Outer Bowl and release it from the machine.
9. Transfer the shake into serving glasses and serve immediately.

Per Serving

Calories: 563 | Fat: 46.3g | Carbs: 16.8g | Fiber: 0.5g | Protein: 6.5g

COOKIE MILKSHAKE

Prep time: 5 minutes | Cook time: 5 minutes | Serves 1

- 1 cup whole milk
- ½ cup amaretto-flavored coffee creamer
- ¼ cup amaretto liqueur
- 1 tablespoon agave nectar
- ¼ cup chopped chocolate chip cookies

1. In a clean Ninja CREAMi pint container, combine the whole milk, coffee creamer, amaretto liqueur, and agave nectar. Stir thoroughly. Secure the lid tightly on the pint container and freeze for at least 24 hours, or until completely solid.
2. After 24 hours, remove the pint container from the freezer and let it sit at room temperature for 5-10 minutes to soften slightly.
3. Place the pint container in the Ninja CREAMi outer bowl, ensuring it is properly locked in place. Install the Creamerizer paddle in the outer bowl lid, and lock the lid assembly onto the outer bowl. Place the bowl assembly on the motor base and twist the handle to the right to secure it in position.
4. Select the "Milkshake" function and press start.
5. After the cycle is complete, remove the lid. Using a spoon, create a 1 ½-inch-wide hole in the center of the milkshake. Add the chopped chocolate chip cookies to the hole, replace the lid, and select the "Mix-In" function.
6. Serve immediately.

Per Serving

Calories: 356 | Protein: 16g | Carbs: 58g | Fiber: 1g | Fat: 7g

CHAPTER 7: ICE CREAM MIX-INS

SNACK MIX ICE CREAM

Prep time: 5 minutes | **Cook time:** 10 seconds | **Serves** 4

- 1 tablespoon cream cheese, softened
- ⅓ cup granulated sugar
- ½ teaspoon vanilla extract
- 1 cup whole milk

- ¾ cup heavy cream
- 2 tablespoons sugar cone pieces
- 1 tablespoon mini pretzels
- 1 tablespoon potato chips, crushed

1. In a large microwave-safe bowl, add the softened cream cheese and microwave on high for about 10 seconds.
2. Remove from the microwave and stir until smooth.
3. Add the granulated sugar and vanilla extract, and using a wire whisk, beat until the mixture resembles frosting.
4. Slowly add the whole milk and heavy cream, and beat until well combined.
5. Transfer the mixture into an empty Ninja CREAMi pint container.
6. Secure the lid and freeze for at least 24 hours.
7. After 24 hours, remove the lid and place the pint container into the Ninja CREAMi outer bowl. Install the Creamerizer Paddle into the outer bowl lid.
8. Lock the lid by rotating it clockwise.
9. Turn the Ninja CREAMi on, and press the "ICE CREAM" button.
10. Once the cycle is complete, use a spoon to create a 1 ½-inch wide hole in the center of the ice cream, reaching the bottom of the pint container.
11. Add the sugar cone pieces, mini pretzels, and crushed potato chips into the hole. Press the "MIX-IN" button.
12. Once the cycle is complete, remove the outer bowl from the Ninja CREAMi.
13. Transfer the ice cream to serving bowls and serve immediately.

Per Serving

Calories: 265 | **Fat: 18g** | **Carbs: 22g** | **Fiber: 0.5g** | **Protein: 5g**

PEANUT BUTTER & JELLY ICE CREAM

Prep time: 15 minutes | **Cook time:** 15 minutes | **Serves** 4

- 3 tablespoons granulated sugar
- 4 large egg yolks
- 1 cup whole milk
- 1/3 cup heavy cream
- ¼ cup smooth peanut butter
- 3 tablespoons grape jelly
- ¼ cup honey roasted peanuts, chopped

1. In a small saucepan, combine the granulated sugar and egg yolks. Whisk until the sugar is dissolved.
2. Add the whole milk, heavy cream, peanut butter, and grape jelly to the saucepan. Stir to combine.
3. Place the saucepan over medium heat and cook, stirring continuously with a rubber spatula, until the mixture reaches 165-175°F.
4. Remove from the heat and strain the mixture through a fine-mesh strainer into an empty Ninja CREAMi pint container.
5. Place the pint container in an ice bath to cool completely.
6. Once cooled, secure the lid and freeze for at least 24 hours.
7. After 24 hours, remove the lid and place the pint container into the Ninja CREAMi outer bowl. Install the Creamerizer Paddle into the outer bowl lid.
8. Lock the lid by rotating it clockwise.
9. Turn the Ninja CREAMi on, and press the "ICE CREAM" button.
10. Once the cycle is complete, use a spoon to create a 1 ½-inch wide hole in the center of the ice cream, reaching the bottom of the pint container.
11. Add the chopped honey roasted peanuts into the hole. Press the "MIX-IN" button.
12. Once the cycle is complete, remove the outer bowl from the Ninja CREAMi.
13. Transfer the ice cream to serving bowls and serve immediately.

Per Serving

Calories: 349 | **Fat:** 23.1g | **Carbs:** 27.5g | **Fiber:** 2g | **Protein:** 11.5g

PEAS AND BERRIES ICE CREAM

Prep time: 5 minutes | Cook time: 10 minutes | Serves 4

- ½ cup frozen peas, thawed
- 3 tablespoons grape jam
- ¾ cup whole milk
- ¼ cup granulated sugar
- 1 teaspoon vanilla extract
- ½ cup heavy cream
- ¼ cup frozen mixed berries
- 2 tablespoons peanut butter powder
- 7 drops purple gel food coloring
- ¼ cup roasted peanuts, chopped

1. In a blender, combine the thawed peas, grape jam, whole milk, granulated sugar, peanut butter powder, food coloring, and vanilla extract. Blend until smooth.
2. Pour the mixture into an empty Ninja CREAMi pint container.
3. Add the heavy cream and stir thoroughly.
4. Secure the lid and freeze for at least 24 hours.
5. After 24 hours, remove the lid and place the pint container into the Ninja CREAMi outer bowl. Install the Creamerizer Paddle into the outer bowl lid.
6. Lock the lid by rotating it clockwise. Turn the Ninja CREAMi on, and press the "ICE CREAM" button.
7. Once the cycle is complete, use a spoon to create a wide hole in the center of the ice cream, reaching the bottom of the pint container.
8. Add the chopped roasted peanuts and frozen mixed berries into the hole. Press the "MIX-IN" button.
9. Scoop the ice cream into serving bowls and serve immediately.

Per Serving

Calories: 202 | Fat: 11g | Carbs: 22g | Fiber: 3g |Protein: 8g

CARAMEL PRETZEL CRUNCH MIX-IN

Prep time: 10 minutes | Cook time: 15 minutes |Serves 4

- 1 pint prepared caramel ice cream
- ¼ cup gluten-free pretzels, crushed
- 2 tablespoons caramel sauce

1. Prepare and freeze your caramel ice cream in the Ninja CREAMi following the standard process (blend base, freeze 24 hours, process on ICE CREAM setting).
2. Once frozen, remove the lid and place the pint container into the Ninja CREAMi outer bowl.
3. Install the Creamerizer Paddle into the outer bowl lid, and lock the lid by rotating it clockwise.
4. Turn the Ninja CREAMi on.
5. Press the "MIX-IN" button.
6. Add the crushed gluten-free pretzels and drizzle the caramel sauce over the ice cream.
7. Run the "MIX-IN" cycle.
8. Once complete, remove the outer bowl from the Ninja CREAMi.
9. Scoop and serve immediately.

Per Serving

Calories: 320 | Fat: 11.4g | Carbs: 50.2g | Fiber: 1.5g | Protein: 5.9g

CHAI TEA ICE CREAM

Prep time: 5 minutes | Cook time: 20 minutes | Serves 4

- 3 cups whole milk, or more to taste
- 3 cups heavy cream
- 3 cups granulated sugar
- 4 cinnamon sticks
- 4 tablespoons loose leaf Indian-style black tea
- 3 tablespoons garam masala (Indian spice blend)
- 10 whole black peppercorns
- 6 cardamom pods
- 2 whole star anise pods
- 1 teaspoon ground nutmeg
- 1 tablespoon vanilla extract
- 1 cup chopped semi-sweet chocolate

1. Combine the whole milk, heavy cream, granulated sugar, cinnamon sticks, black tea, garam masala, peppercorns, cardamom pods, star anise pods, and nutmeg in a saucepan. Bring to a simmer and cook for 20 minutes.
2. Strain the mixture through a fine-mesh strainer into a large bowl. Add up to 1 cup more whole milk to adjust the spice level and sweetness to your preference.
3. Pour the mixture into a Ninja CREAMi pint container. Secure the lid and freeze for at least 24 hours.
4. After 24 hours, place the frozen pint container into the Ninja CREAMi outer bowl. Install the Creamerizer Paddle into the outer bowl lid. Lock the lid by rotating it clockwise.
5. Turn the Ninja CREAMi on, and press the "ICE CREAM" button.
6. Once the cycle is complete, use a spoon to create a 1 ½-inch wide hole in the center of the ice cream, reaching the bottom of the pint container.
7. Add the chopped semi-sweet chocolate to the hole, and press the "MIX-IN" button.
8. Once the cycle is complete, scoop the ice cream into serving bowls and serve immediately.

Per Serving

Calories: 515 | Fat: 34g | Carbs: 49g | Fiber: 2g | Protein: 6g

VANILLA BLUEBERRY ICE CREAM

Prep time: 10 minutes | Cook time: 10 minutes | Serves 6

- 6 pre-made pie crust cups (optional, for serving)
- 1 cup whole milk
- ¾ cup heavy cream
- ⅓ cup granulated sugar
- 1 large egg, beaten
- ½ cup frozen blueberries, thawed

1. Combine the whole milk, heavy cream, granulated sugar, beaten egg, and thawed blueberries in a blender. Blend until smooth.
2. Pour the mixture into a Ninja CREAMi pint container, and secure the lid.
3. Freeze the pint container for at least 24 hours.
4. Once frozen, remove the lid from the pint container. Place the pint container into the Ninja CREAMi outer bowl. Install the Creamerizer Paddle into the outer bowl lid.
5. Lock the lid by rotating it clockwise.
6. Turn the Ninja CREAMi on, and press the "ICE CREAM" button.
7. Once the cycle is complete, remove the outer bowl from the Ninja CREAMi.
8. Serve immediately. For a fun presentation, serve in pre-made pie crust cups.

Per Serving

Calories: 109.5 | Fat: 70g | Carbs: 103.3g | Fiber: 3.4g | Protein: 14.3g

LAVENDER COOKIES AND CREAM DELIGHT

Prep Time: 10 minutes | Cook time: 30 minutes | Serves 2

- ½ cup heavy cream
- ½ tablespoon dried lavender
- ½ cup whole milk
- ¼ cup sweetened condensed milk
- 2 drops purple food coloring
- ¼ cup crushed chocolate wafer cookies

1. Whisk together the heavy cream and dried lavender in a medium saucepan.
2. Steep the mixture over low heat for 10 minutes, stirring every 2 minutes to prevent bubbling.
3. Strain the lavender from the heavy cream through a fine-mesh strainer into a large mixing bowl. Discard the lavender.
4. In a separate large mixing bowl, combine the whole milk, sweetened condensed milk, and purple food coloring. Whisk until smooth.
5. Pour the base into an empty Ninja CREAMi pint container. Place the pint container in an ice bath to cool completely. Once cooled, secure the lid and freeze for at least 24 hours.
6. After 24 hours, remove the lid and place the pint container into the Ninja CREAMi outer bowl. Install the Creamerizer Paddle into the outer bowl lid. Lock the lid by rotating it clockwise. Turn the Ninja CREAMi on, and press the "ICE CREAM" button.
7. Once the cycle is complete, use a spoon to create a 1 ½-inch wide hole in the center of the ice cream, reaching the bottom of the pint container. Add the crushed chocolate wafer cookies to the hole, and press the "MIX-IN" button.
8. Once the cycle is complete, scoop the ice cream into serving bowls and serve immediately, topped with extra crumbled wafers if desired.

Per Serving

Calories: 545 | Fat:2g | Carbs:4g | Protein:23g | Fiber: 1g

STRAWBERRY SHORTCAKE MIX-IN

Prep time: 10 minutes | Cook time: 15 minutes |Serves 4

- 1 pint prepared vanilla ice cream
- ¼ cup gluten-free shortbread cookies, crumbled
- ¼ cup fresh strawberries, diced

1. Prepare and freeze your vanilla ice cream in the Ninja CREAMi following the standard process (blend base, freeze 24 hours, process on ICE CREAM setting).
2. Once frozen, remove the lid and place the pint container into the Ninja CREAMi outer bowl.
3. Install the Creamerizer Paddle into the outer bowl lid, and lock the lid by rotating it clockwise.
4. Turn the Ninja CREAMi on.
5. Press the "MIX-IN" button.
6. Add the crumbled shortbread cookies and diced strawberries.
7. Run the "MIX-IN" cycle.
8. Once complete, remove the outer bowl from the Ninja CREAMi.
9. Scoop and serve immediately.

Per Serving

Calories: 285 | Fat: 9.6g | | Carbs: 45.7g | Fiber: 2.3g | Protein: 6.1g

VANILLA ICE CREAM WITH CHOCOLATE CHIPS

Prep time: 5 minutes | Cook time: 5 minutes | Serves 4

- 1 tablespoon cream cheese, softened
- ⅓ cup granulated sugar
- 1 teaspoon vanilla extract
- ¾ cup heavy cream
- 1 cup whole milk
- ¼ cup mini chocolate chips, for mix-in

1. Microwave the softened cream cheese for 10 seconds in a large microwave-safe bowl. Using a rubber spatula, blend in the granulated sugar and vanilla extract until the mixture resembles frosting, about 60 seconds.
2. Slowly whisk in the heavy cream and whole milk until smooth and the sugar has dissolved.
3. Pour the base into an empty Ninja CREAMi pint container. Secure the lid and freeze for at least 24 hours.
4. After 24 hours, remove the lid and place the pint container into the Ninja CREAMi outer bowl. Install the Creamerizer Paddle into the outer bowl lid. Lock the lid by rotating it clockwise. Turn the Ninja CREAMi on, and press the "ICE CREAM" button.
5. Once the cycle is complete, use a spoon to create a 1 ½-inch wide hole in the center of the ice cream, reaching the bottom of the pint container.

Add the mini chocolate chips to the hole, and press the "MIX-IN" button.
6. Once the cycle is complete, scoop the ice cream into serving bowls and serve immediately.

Per Serving

Calories: 285 | Fat: 19g | Carbs: 23g | Fiber: 1g | Protein: 6g

RADICAL ROCKY ROAD ICE CREAM

Prep time: 5 minutes | Cook time: 50 minutes | Serves 6

- 2 cups heavy cream
- 1 cup whole milk
- ¾ cup granulated sugar
- 1 tablespoon vanilla extract
- ½ cup unsweetened cocoa powder
- ½ cup chopped pecans
- 1 cup mini marshmallows

1. In a large mixing bowl, combine the heavy cream, whole milk, granulated sugar, vanilla extract, and unsweetened cocoa powder. Whisk until the sugar and cocoa powder are fully dissolved and the mixture is smooth.
2. Pour the mixture into a Ninja CREAMi pint container. Secure the lid.
3. Freeze the pint container for at least 24 hours.
4. After 24 hours, remove the lid and place the frozen pint container into the Ninja CREAMi outer bowl. Install the Creamerizer Paddle into the outer bowl lid.
5. Lock the lid by rotating it clockwise.
6. Turn the Ninja CREAMi on, and press the "ICE CREAM" button.
7. Once the cycle is complete, use a spoon to create a 1 ½-inch wide hole in the center of the ice cream, reaching the bottom of the pint container.
8. Add the chopped pecans and mini marshmallows to the hole. Press the "MIX-IN" button.
9. Once the cycle is complete, scoop the ice cream into serving bowls and serve immediately.

Per Serving

Calories: 418 | Fat: 36g | Carbs: 26g | Fiber: 3g | Protein: 5g

FRUITY CEREAL ICE CREAM

Prep time: 5 minutes | Cook time: 30 minutes | Serves 2

- ¾ cup whole milk
- 1 cup fruity cereal, divided
- 1 tablespoon cream cheese, softened
- ¼ cup granulated sugar
- 1 teaspoon vanilla extract
- ½ cup heavy cream

1. In a large mixing bowl, combine ½ cup of the fruity cereal and the whole milk. Allow the mixture to steep for 15-30 minutes, stirring occasionally to infuse the milk with the fruity flavor.
2. Microwave the softened cream cheese for 10 seconds in a separate microwave-safe bowl. In a mixing bowl, combine the granulated sugar and vanilla extract, and whisk or use a rubber spatula until the mixture resembles frosting, about 60 seconds.
3. After 15-30 minutes, strain the milk and cereal mixture through a fine-mesh strainer into the bowl with the sugar mixture. Press on the cereal with a spoon to extract extra milk, then discard the cereal. Mix in the heavy cream until thoroughly combined.
4. Pour the mixture into an empty Ninja CREAMi pint container. Secure the lid and freeze for at least 24 hours.
5. After 24 hours, remove the lid and place the pint container into the Ninja CREAMi outer bowl. Install the Creamerizer Paddle into the outer bowl lid.
6. Lock the lid by rotating it clockwise. Turn the Ninja CREAMi on, and press the "ICE CREAM" button.
7. Once the cycle is complete, use a spoon to create a 1 ½-inch wide hole in the center of the ice cream, reaching the bottom of the pint container. Add the remaining ½ cup of fruity cereal to the hole, and press the "MIX-IN" button.
8. Once the cycle is complete, scoop the ice cream into serving bowls and serve immediately.

Per Serving

Calories: 312 | Fat: 18g | Carbs: 32g | Fiber: 1g | Protein: 5g

CHOCOLATE SNOW ICE CREAM

Prep time: 5 minutes | Cook time: 20 minutes | Serves 4

- 2 cups milk (whole or plant-based)
- 1 cup confectioners' sugar
- 1 tablespoon vanilla extract
- ¼ cup unsweetened cocoa powder
- 1 teaspoon instant coffee powder
- 1 cup crushed ice (to mimic snow texture, use sparingly)

1. In a large bowl, whisk together the milk, confectioners' sugar, vanilla extract, cocoa powder, and instant coffee powder until the sugar has dissolved and the mixture is smooth.
2. Add the crushed ice to the mixture. Be careful not to add too much, as it will make the ice cream very icy.
3. Pour the mixture into a Ninja CREAMi pint container. Secure the lid.
4. Freeze the pint container for at least 24 hours.
5. After 24 hours, remove the lid and place the frozen pint container into the Ninja CREAMi outer bowl. Install the Creamerizer Paddle into the outer bowl lid.
6. Lock the lid by rotating it clockwise.
7. Turn the Ninja CREAMi on, and press the "SLUSHIE" or "SORBET" button (depending on your desired consistency). If needed, use the "RE-SPIN" function.
8. Scoop and serve immediately.

Per Serving

Calories: 210 | Fat: 6g | Carbs: 37g | Fiber: 2g | Protein: 4g

MINT CHOCOLATE CHIP ICE CREAM

Prep time: 5 minutes | Cook time: 5 minutes | Serves 4

- 1 tablespoon cream cheese, softened
- ⅓ cup granulated sugar
- 1 teaspoon vanilla extract
- ¾ cup heavy cream
- 1 cup whole milk
- 1 teaspoon mint extract
- Green food coloring (optional)
- ¼ cup mini chocolate chips, for mix-in

1. Microwave the softened cream cheese for 10 seconds in a large microwave-safe bowl. Combine with the granulated sugar and mint extract, and using a whisk or rubber spatula, mix for about 60 seconds or until the mixture resembles frosting.
2. Slowly whisk in the heavy cream, whole milk, and optional green food coloring until thoroughly mixed and the sugar has dissolved.
3. Pour the base into an empty Ninja CREAMi pint container. Secure the lid and freeze for at least 24 hours.
4. After 24 hours, remove the lid and place the pint container into the Ninja CREAMi outer bowl. Install the Creamerizer Paddle into the outer bowl lid. Lock the lid by rotating it clockwise. Turn the Ninja CREAMi on, and press the "ICE CREAM" button.
5. Once the cycle is complete, use a spoon to create a 1 ½-inch wide hole in the center of the ice cream, reaching the bottom of the pint container. Add the mini chocolate chips to the hole, and press the "MIX-IN" button.
6. Once the cycle is complete, scoop the ice cream into serving bowls and serve immediately.

Per Serving

Calories: 275 | Fat: 19g | Carbs: 22g | Fiber: 1g | Protein: 4g

PISTACHIO ICE CREAM

Prep time: 5 minutes | Cook time: 3 minutes | Serves 4

- 1 tablespoon cream cheese, softened
- ⅓ cup granulated sugar
- 1 teaspoon almond extract
- 1 cup whole milk
- ¾ cup heavy cream
- ¼ cup pistachios, shelled and chopped

1. In a large microwave-safe bowl, microwave the softened cream cheese on high for about 10 seconds.
2. Remove from the microwave and stir until smooth.
3. Add the granulated sugar and almond extract, and using a wire whisk, beat until the mixture resembles frosting.
4. Slowly add the whole milk and heavy cream, and beat until well combined.
5. Transfer the mixture into an empty Ninja CREAMi pint container.
6. Secure the lid and freeze for at least 24 hours.
7. After 24 hours, remove the lid and place the pint container into the Ninja CREAMi outer bowl. Install the Creamerizer Paddle into the outer bowl lid.
8. Lock the lid by rotating it clockwise.
9. Turn the Ninja CREAMi on, and press the "ICE CREAM" button.
10. Once the cycle is complete, use a spoon to create a 1 ½-inch wide hole in the center of the ice cream, reaching the bottom of the pint container.
11. Add the chopped pistachios into the hole. Press the "MIX-IN" button.
12. Once the cycle is complete, remove the outer bowl from the Ninja CREAMi.
13. Transfer the ice cream to serving bowls and serve immediately.

Per Serving

Calories: 285 | Fat: 20g | Carbs: 21g | Fiber: 2g | Protein: 4g

CAROB CHIP MINT SOY VANILLA VEGAN ICE CREAM

Prep time: 5 minutes | **Cook time: 35 minutes** | **Makes 1 quart**

- 1 pound silken tofu
- ½ cup plus 2 tablespoons granulated sugar
- ½ teaspoon kosher salt
- 1 vanilla bean, split lengthwise
- ¾ cup virgin coconut oil, melted and slightly cooled
- 1 cup vegan carob chips
- ¼ cup fresh mint leaves, finely chopped

1. Place the silken tofu, granulated sugar, and kosher salt in a blender. Scrape the seeds from the vanilla bean into the blender. Puree the mixture until smooth, about 15 seconds. With the blender on medium speed, slowly drizzle in the melted and slightly cooled coconut oil. Blend until the mixture is thick, but do not over-blend.
2. Pour the mixture into a Ninja CREAMi pint container. Secure the lid.
3. Freeze the pint container for at least 24 hours.
4. After 24 hours, remove the lid and place the frozen pint container into the Ninja CREAMi outer bowl. Install the Creamerizer Paddle into the outer bowl lid.
5. Lock the lid by rotating it clockwise.
6. Turn the Ninja CREAMi on, and press the "ICE CREAM" button.
7. Once the cycle is complete, use a spoon to create a 1 ½-inch wide hole in the center of the ice cream, reaching the bottom of the pint container.
8. Add the vegan carob chips and finely chopped mint leaves to the hole. Press the "MIX-IN" button.
9. Once the cycle is complete, scoop and serve immediately.

Per Serving

Calories: 322 | **Fat: 24g** | **Carbs: 28g** | **Fiber: 4g** | **Protein: 5g**

GRASSHOPPER ICE CREAM

Prep time: 5 minutes | Cook time: 3 minutes | Serves 4

- ½ cup frozen spinach, thawed and squeezed dry
- 1 cup whole milk
- ½ cup granulated sugar
- 1 teaspoon mint extract
- 3-5 drops green food coloring
- ⅓ cup heavy cream
- ¼ cup chocolate chunks, chopped
- ¼ cup brownie, cut into 1-inch pieces

1. In a high-speed blender, combine the thawed spinach, whole milk, granulated sugar, mint extract, and green food coloring. Pulse until smooth.
2. Transfer the mixture into an empty Ninja CREAMi pint container.
3. Add the heavy cream and stir until well combined.
4. Secure the lid and freeze for at least 24 hours.
5. After 24 hours, remove the lid and place the pint container into the Ninja CREAMi outer bowl. Install the Creamerizer Paddle into the outer bowl lid.
6. Lock the lid by rotating it clockwise.
7. Turn the Ninja CREAMi on, and press the "ICE CREAM" button.
8. Once the cycle is complete, use a spoon to create a 1 ½-inch wide hole in the center of the ice cream, reaching the bottom of the pint container.
9. Add the chopped chocolate chunks and brownie pieces into the hole. Press the "MIX-IN" button.
10. Once the cycle is complete, remove the outer bowl from the Ninja CREAMi.
11. Transfer the ice cream to serving bowls and serve immediately.

Per Serving

Calories: 295 | Fat: 21g | Carbs: 23g | Fiber: 2g | Protein: 4g

MEASUREMENT CONVERSION CHART

VOLUME EQUIVALENTS(DRY)

US STANDARD	METRIC (APPROXIMATE)
1/8 teaspoon	0.5 mL
1/4 teaspoon	1 mL
1/2 teaspoon	2 mL
3/4 teaspoon	4 mL
1 teaspoon	5 mL
1 tablespoon	15 mL
1/4 cup	59 mL
1/2 cup	118 mL
3/4 cup	177 mL
1 cup	235 mL
2 cups	475 mL
3 cups	700 mL
4 cups	1 L

WEIGHT EQUIVALENTS

US STANDARD	METRIC (APPROXIMATE)
1 ounce	28 g
2 ounces	57 g
5 ounces	142 g
10 ounces	284 g
15 ounces	425 g
16 ounces (1 pound)	455 g
1.5 pounds	680 g
2 pounds	907 g

VOLUME EQUIVALENTS(LIQUID)

US STANDARD	US STANDARD (OUNCES)	METRIC (APPROXIMATE)
2 tablespoons	1 fl.oz.	30 mL
1/4 cup	2 fl.oz.	60 mL
1/2 cup	4 fl.oz.	120 mL
1 cup	8 fl.oz.	240 mL
1 1/2 cup	12 fl.oz.	355 mL
2 cups or 1 pint	16 fl.oz.	475 mL
4 cups or 1 quart	32 fl.oz.	1 L
1 gallon	128 fl.oz.	4 L

TEMPERATURES EQUIVALENTS

FAHRENHEIT(F)	CELSIUS(C) (APPROXIMATE)
225 °F	107 °C
250 °F	120 °C
275 °F	135 °C
300 °F	150 °C
325 °F	160 °C
350 °F	180 °C
375 °F	190 °C
400 °F	205 °C
425 °F	220 °C
450 °F	235 °C
475 °F	245 °C
500 °F	260 °C

The Dirty Dozen and Clean Fifteen

The Environmental Working Group (EWG) is a nonprofit, nonpartisan organization dedicated to protecting human health and the environment Its mission is to empower people to live healthier lives in a healthier environment. This organization publishes an annual list of the twelve kinds of produce, in sequence, that have the highest amount of pesticide residue-the Dirty Dozen-as well as a list of the fifteen kinds ofproduce that have the least amount of pesticide residue-the Clean Fifteen.

THE DIRTY DOZEN

- The 2016 Dirty Dozen includes the following produce. These are considered among the year's most important produce to buy organic:

Strawberries	Spinach
Apples	Tomatoes
Nectarines	Bell peppers
Peaches	Cherry tomatoes
Celery	Cucumbers
Grapes	Kale/collard greens
Cherries	Hot peppers

- *The Dirty Dozen list contains two additional itemskale/collard greens and hot peppers-because they tend to contain trace levels of highly hazardous pesticides.*

THE CLEAN FIFTEEN

- The least critical to buy organically are the Clean Fifteen list. The following are on the 2016 list:

Avocados	Papayas
Corn	Kiw
Pineapples	Eggplant
Cabbage	Honeydew
Sweet peas	Grapefruit
Onions	Cantaloupe
Asparagus	Cauliflower
Mangos	

- *Some of the sweet corn sold in the United States are made from genetically engineered (GE) seedstock. Buy organic varieties of these crops to avoid GE produce.*

APPENDIX 3: INDEX

Hey there!

Wow, can you believe we've reached the end of this culinary journey together? I'm truly thrilled and filled with joy as I think back on all the recipes we've shared and the flavors we've discovered. This experience, blending a bit of tradition with our own unique twists, has been a journey of love for good food. And knowing you've been out there, giving these dishes a try, has made this adventure incredibly special to me.

Even though we're turning the last page of this book, I hope our conversation about all things delicious doesn't have to end. I cherish your thoughts, your experiments, and yes, even those moments when things didn't go as planned. Every piece of feedback you share is invaluable, helping to enrich this experience for us all.

I'd be so grateful if you could take a moment to share your thoughts with me, be it through a review on Amazon or any other place you feel comfortable expressing yourself online. Whether it's praise, constructive criticism, or even an idea for how we might do things differently in the future, your input is what truly makes this journey meaningful.

This book is a piece of my heart, offered to you with all the love and enthusiasm I have for cooking. But it's your engagement and your words that elevate it to something truly extraordinary.

Thank you from the bottom of my heart for being such an integral part of this culinary adventure. Your openness to trying new things and sharing your experiences has been the greatest gift.

Catch you later,

Kelly R. Bonilla

Printed in Great Britain
by Amazon

62264763R00045